An Artist's Odyssey

Praise for *An Artist's Odyssey*

"I was captivated by Sarkis Antikajian's relaxed, intimate storytelling and couldn't put the book down until I reached the end. Sarkis invites the reader on his journey to fulfill his lifelong dream of becoming an artist. You will rejoice in his success and feel his frustration with setbacks and, ultimately, find his love of painting and joie de vivre thoroughly addictive."

—Wyatt Burger, pianist and teacher

"The world is full of people who hear the muse but never heed the message. Sarkis Antikajian heard it clearly. Despite decades of delay and discouragement that should have forever blocked the message, he answered the call and forged a life as a respected, successful artist."

—Mike Thoele, author of *Footprints Across Oregon* and *Fire Line: Summer Battles of the West*

"A compelling, in-depth look at Sarkis Antikajian's lengthy journey to become an artist. It is a story fraught with obstacles that would have deterred most people. He chased his dream and faced the challenges with courage and determination to become the amazing artist he is today. I highly recommend this inspirational memoir to anyone who loves art or is pursuing a dream."

—Robert Young, award-winning author of twenty-eight books, including *Lobo: The Hunted and the Hunter*

"Sarkis Antikajian's inspiring memoir is a testament of perseverance in the pursuit of our dreams. With a resolute commitment we can overcome any obstacle to reach our goals."

—Sunny Apinchapong-Yang, artist and author of *Intuitive Painting: A Retrospective*

"Painting and writing share common criteria essential for excellence in creating art: observation, emotion, and expression. In this memoir, Sarkis Antikajian's words tell of his childhood quest for an artistic life. It's a vivid insight into his long and rich life of overcoming obstacles to become the expressive colorful artist and writer he is."

—Guido Frick, painter and writer

"I have admired Sarkis Antikajian's art for years. He has been my inspiration and my mentor. We are fortunate that he has shared his captivating long journey to become the accomplished painter that he is."

—Chrissie Forbes, artist and teacher

An Artist's Odyssey

From Dream to Reality

SARKIS ANTIKAJIAN

SA Studio Press

CHESHIRE, OREGON

SA Studio Press
Cheshire, Oregon
Copyright © 2024 by Sarkis Antikajian.

Library of Congress Control Number: 2024903023
Print ISBN: 979-8-218-34123-7
E-book ISBN: 979-8-218-34124-4

Book cover and interior design by Christina Thiele
Cover art, *Self-Portrait*, Sarkis Antikajian
Editorial production by kn literary

sarkisantikajian.com

To my sons, Kyle and Garrick, whose presence in my world made it complete.

To Karen, my loving wife and companion of sixty-three years who shared with me moments that brightened my outlook on life, and stood by me when disappointments dimmed my day-to-day happiness.

Contents

PART I

JORDAN

CHAPTER 1

How It Began

It's December 2, 2021. I am on the last page of the novel I've been reading for the last two weeks: Lust for Life *by Irving Stone, based on the life of Vincent Van Gogh. It was published in 1934, a year after my birth. The book had popped up on Amazon as a "recommended book for Sarkis Antikajian," a marketing ploy triggered by my interest in art and books on artists. As I cradle the novel between my arthritic, gnarled fingers, my thoughts travel to a faraway country, to a different time.*

———

I was fifteen in 1948, the year I discovered by chance, at the end of a shelf at the United States Information Service library in Amman, Jordan, an art book on French impressionist and post-impressionist artists. Next to it, the novel *Lust for Life*. No one was around except for the librarian, who sat at his desk, reading a book. I set the two books on a table and leafed through the art book for over an hour, fascinated by what I saw: dazzling paintings of the French countryside, of streams, meadows, and woodlands that I couldn't imagine existed in real life. Vincent Van Gogh's sunflower still life glowed. Looking at his pointillist self-portrait, I felt I was in his presence. I read, over and over, a few snippets of letters he wrote to his brother, Theo, and through those letters, I learned of Van Gogh's successes, but even more of his tribulations. Within an hour, he had become my idol. The librarian at the checkout counter looked over the volumes in my hands and smiled.

At home in my bedroom, captivated by what I saw in the art book pages, I drifted like a runaway balloon afloat in a breezy sky over imaginary woodlands, pastures, and hills. I pored over the fascinating novel, comparing the various artists' works it mentioned with images of those works in the art book. I walked along with them in the streets of Paris, listening to their heated arguments, feeling their passion and insecurities. With Gauguin, I experienced the jungles of Tahiti and watched him paint a golden, semi-nude Polynesian woman. I sat next to Toulouse-Lautrec while he deftly drew the voluptuous dancers at the Moulin Rouge. I trudged the countryside with Van Gogh as he painted spring's blossoming orchards; gnarled, ashen olive trees; and whirling cypress trees.

During the next few weeks, I read the novel twice. And through these two books, I befriended those artists and felt their passion, shared their personalities and the magic of their creations—each so individual—and I was determined to be one of them. Through Van Gogh's letters and the rugged quality of his paintings, I lived his passion and adopted his philosophy of art. I told myself I would give anything to paint like him. Ever since, Vincent Van Gogh has dominated my artistic psyche.

Watching American movies in my adolescence, I had fantasies of becoming a flamenco guitarist playing an alegrías in a cozy bar while a gorgeous dancer struck the floor with her heels; a matador swirling his red cape challenging a bull; a cowboy on the Wyoming prairie, galloping with grace as one entity with his quarter horse; Rudolph Valentino seducing young women in an elegant tango; and many others. Because of my introverted disposition and lack of physical prowess, I knew they would remain mere fantasies. Yet the life of the artist I envisioned while reading the novel and poring over the images in the art book was a perfect fit for my personality. The novel and the art book spawned a fantasy. Its appeal was so captivating it morphed into a steadfast obsession.

Between the ages of nine and twelve, on weekdays, I lived with my sister Aleece and her husband, Vahan, in the Armenian Quarter of the Old City of Jerusalem. I attended Terra Sancta College, an elementary and secondary American-Franciscan private school in the New City of Jerusalem. I spent weekends at our home in Amman.

On Sunday afternoons, sandwiched between strangers in a rickety taxicab, I traveled the winding highway from Amman, through the town of As-Salt, through Jericho, to Jerusalem. With every bump and swerve in the suffocating heat, I was on the verge of throwing up.

Aleece and Vahan did their utmost to make me feel at home in a serene environment, yet throughout those weekdays, I was homesick, bored, and lonely. Of the years I spent in Jerusalem, I have no memory of my teachers or the nature of my studies. The thought of attending school, subjected to what I had no interest in, always bred anxieties. Yet early on, I knew it was possible to do well in school or in any venture if I had a purpose. And my purpose, despite my lack of interest in my studies, was to excel in order to please my parents and not let them down.

My sister and Vahan gave me leeway to spend time on my own, which suited me well. As a relief from my tedious schoolwork, I discovered a pleasurable activity. With a pencil and paper, I copied photos of Armenian priests from religious pamphlets. The process was a challenge, yet I immersed myself in my rudimentary artistic journey, captivated by the activity itself. With perseverance, going through the process of trial and error, of drawing and erasing, I tortured the pieces of paper to reach a satisfactory outcome. Drawing gave me an enormous satisfaction, which made the tedious schoolwork tolerable. And so, over time, drawing filled the solitary life I chose—a preferred state that followed me throughout my adult life.

When the Arab Israeli conflict heated in Palestine, my parents wanted me home. Terra Sancta College had established a branch in Amman, which allowed me to continue my high school education while living at home.

Until I was in high school, I had no access to books other than my textbooks—not even newspapers. Then Mr. Butrus, a charismatic history and English teacher, introduced us to the United States Information Service library, which, to my knowledge, was the only library in Amman at the time that carried books written in English. Mr. Butrus was a man some students hated and others admired. Elementary school students envisaged his presence in their lives, some with curiosity and others with apprehension.

In his English class, he introduced us to the classics and inspired us to read. I learned how to comprehend and value even the most cumbersome first two hundred pages of a foreign novel, such as those of Dostoevsky and Tolstoy, to find myself immersed in the most fascinating narrative.

Just as captivating was Butrus's mesmerizing portrayal of historical events. His words were so real, I almost imagined he had experienced it all, that he may have lived through those bygone years, and that he may have known the people he described, whether Napoleon, Bismarck, or an urchin roaming the streets of Paris at the time of the French Revolution. Sometimes, halting his narrative, he would scan every one of us with a glow in his eyes, demanding close attention. "Just wait," he appeared to tell us. "In a moment, I am going to tell you the most fascinating story." Facing us, he would pace back and forth, and as his enthusiasm rose, he would pick on his dry lips until they bled. Yet his voice resonated without betraying a hint of discomfort. And thus, in his lectures, he introduced me to curious worlds.

In a country oblivious to what went on in the rest of the world, books offered me a mental escape to faraway places.

CHAPTER 2

A Taste of the Real

Intoxicated by what I saw in art books, gripped by the fantasy that one day I, too, would become an artist, with a No. 2 pencil and a lined notebook intended for words, I immersed myself in drawing sprees. I drew almost everything in sight: our black German shepherd, a caterpillar slinking over deep green leaves, a turtle with its bony ochre-and-umber patterned home that wandered into our garden, a writhing sienna centipede, a black millipede I imagined as a train without an engine or a caboose.

I borrowed the art book from the library a few times. The more I leafed through the pages, imprinting the fascinating artwork in my mind, the more I became determined to someday be a painter.

In 1950, my sister Alexandra and her husband, Joseph, stayed with us for a few days. Although Joseph was a bookkeeper, he was also a dreamer who wanted to be a writer, a photographer, and a painter. He had corresponded with an American woman who, knowing of his interest in painting, sent him an artist box of oil paints, a couple of brushes, a wooden palette, and a yard or two of primed canvas, which he had brought with him to our home.

One morning, he set up a still life of a bundle of grapes from our grapevine, a vase of flowers from our garden, and a pear. He squeezed globs of oil paint around the periphery of his palette—dazzling yellow, red, green, blue, purple, and white—and began to paint. Until that day, I had never seen or heard of any other living painter. Sitting next to Joseph, I witnessed the process of applying the luscious oil paint to canvas and breathed the seductive scent of linseed oil and turpentine. Brushstroke after brushstroke, images materialized on his canvas.

At some point, piling paint over paint, intermixing the intense colors in his attempt to form the shape and color of the grape bundle, his painting plunged into a muddy and tired-looking state. Frustrated, he decided to scrape off what he had done so as to salvage the precious canvas. In an impulse I asked him if he would let me work on his canvas for a little while. He handed me the brush. Thus, Joseph became instrumental in initiating my artistic journey.

He left me his paint box and canvas. Over the following weeks, I painted copies of landscapes from postcards and chocolate box covers. I even attempted to paint my baby niece sleeping in her crib. With acute focus and determination, brush in hand, I became transfixed with the painting process, sent into a heightened state of self-satisfaction that I had not yet experienced in my life.

When I was eighteen years old, having graduated from the prestigious Franciscan-American high school, I faced a dilemma: What to do with my life.

My brother and my three sisters, all older than me, had not gone to school beyond eighth grade. My brother, Ohanness, eleven years older than me, had married at eighteen and planned to work with my father and someday take over the family transportation business. My three sisters—Aleece, nine years older than me; Peggy, five years older; and Alexandra, two years older—had all married young, even as young as sixteen. Women in that part of the world didn't have meaningful jobs other than being maids. When married, they were housewives taking care of their families.

My parents hoped I'd become a prominent professional in Amman—a physician, an engineer, or a pharmacist—and be their pride and joy: a son with a coveted status in the community. I carried the obligation to fulfill their expectations as a burden.

Both of my parents valued education, something neither of them had an opportunity for. My mother grew up in a poor environment in the Armenian Quarter of the Old City of Jerusalem. She had never been to school. Yet she was an adept seamstress working for the British, who, at the time, had a mandate over Palestine. My father may not have had any meaningful schooling either. He was born to Armenian parents in Gurun, a small village in Turkey. Succumbing to the trauma of losing his family during the Armenian Genocide, what saved him was his skill driving military vehicles. Conscripted as a weaponless driver, he found his way to Palestine. When the Ottomans were defeated by the allies, he stayed behind, married my mother in Jerusalem, and established a lucrative transportation business in Amman, Transjordan. I never saw my father read or write, other than scribbling his illegible signature in Armenian on Arabic written documents.

Living in what I believed to be an unimaginative country, through the books I read I fantasized of faraway places that would give me the opportunity to become the person I aspired to be: an artist. Art, a way of life embedded in me, pulled me onto an imaginary road that had no clear destination. I needed to realize the fantasy that I yearned for.

I knew even then that making art as a vocation wouldn't provide financial independence and I would need the support of someone else, as shown in the lives of the artists in the art book and novel. This meant I would need my parents' indefinite support, and that wasn't an option. It led me to succumb to an impetuous choice of a vocation: studying engineering at the American University of Beirut (AUB) in Beirut, Lebanon.

My mother, Nazouhi
Minassian, born Jerusalem,
Palestine (1892–1968)

My father, Serop Antikajian, born
Gurun, Turkey (1897–1974)

My siblings and me (left to right: Alexandra, Aleece, Sarkis,
Peggy, Ohanness)

CHAPTER 3

A Failed Salesman

Despite my unhappiness with and disinterest in most of the classes I took in pre-engineering, the course I most remember was called General Education. It was a prerequisite all freshman students had to take before proceeding with their major. It introduced us to many fields of study to acquaint us with various vocations that would be helpful in our career decision-making. Presenters shared their expertise in their individual professions. I found all humanities topics interesting, yet the one I enjoyed most and that reinforced my goal was the history of art. It spanned art periods from the Renaissance to German Expressionism. Displaying vivid descriptions and images on a screen, the speaker introduced us to the fascinating prominent artists who represented the various art movements and styles. I listened with utmost interest. Every word enforced my will to become a painter.

It wasn't long until I realized majoring in engineering was a fruitless struggle. I was weak in math, and the meticulous drafting bored me. Yet I knew if I quit my studies altogether, I would be a total failure in my parents' eyes. My father had gone into debt fulfilling their expectations, a responsibility I couldn't discard. But what to do?

The discovery of potash and other important minerals in a village a few kilometers from Amman had the potential to entice foreign chemical companies to invest in Transjordan.

It meant the need for chemists. At my brother's suggestion, I switched my major from engineering to chemistry, with no clue what I'd do with a degree in chemistry once I graduated. Working in a chemical lab didn't seem a bad idea for an introvert. I didn't look forward to living in a small, dusty village for years, even if I gained employment with a foreign chemical company. The plausible path to achieving my desire got dimmer and dimmer. I changed my major to chemistry.

What I remember most of those years as a student at AUB was the university's private rocky beach, where I learned how to swim. Swimming was another prerequisite for graduation that I enjoyed, even though when I stepped on sea urchins prevalent on the rocky beach, their spikes embedded in my feet. My attempt at digging them out with a needle was an excruciating process. Just as troublesome was the occasional jellyfish-covered surface of the water that made the Mediterranean Sea a baby-blue sheet as reflective as glass. When swimming in such an environment, if the tentacles of the jellyfish touched the skin, they caused extreme burning and itching that lasted for a few days.

One memorable class I enrolled in that had nothing to do with chemistry was an evening drawing class. The instructor was a charming young American woman who wore thick-rimmed glasses and drove a small European car. She was one of two American instructors at AUB. There were four of us in the class. In one of the drawing sessions, the assignment was "Keeping Streets Clean." In my pencil sketch, I showed a woman discarding a piece of paper into a sidewalk trash bin. To my surprise, the university's medical school included my sketch in their newsletter. That slight gesture gave me an unforeseen satisfaction—a memorable taste of artistic achievement.

When I returned home after earning my bachelor of science degree in chemistry, I realized two things: the potash industry wouldn't be workable for years to come, and a degree in chemistry provided me only the opportunity to gain employment as a salesperson—a representative of a Swiss medical company.

My job entailed visiting physicians in major towns in Jordan (Emir Abdullah had renamed Transjordan the Kingdom of Jordan), promoting our company's products and citing the advantages of our brand of medical drugs over those of comparative companies. The job required social skills and the ability to project total confidence by conversing with a few concise and convincing words. I had neither.

For two years on my monthly route as a salesman, I dreaded each encounter with physicians. Plagued by anxiety, sweaty hands, and rashes, my work plunged me into misery. Soon I realized I needed to quit my job, agonizingly aware that I had already lost four years in an uneventful blunder at my parents' expense. Quitting my job altogether, with no skill of any kind, limited meaningful employment that would provide me with financial independence.

During the two years I worked as a medical representative, I lived at home. With no expenses to speak of, I gave almost all my wages to my mother to spend as she wished. She was proud to see me dressed in a sport jacket and tie when I went to work. And was impressed by my medical knowledge when I gave her vitamin samples that might ease fissures in the corners of her mouth, all the while insisting she should see a physician. Yet, during my last few months as a medical salesman, it became clear to my mother how unhappy I was with my job.

My mother, a selfless woman, wanted the best for her children. To this day I feel the familiar pang of guilt when I think of the time I was in my teens and asked her to wake me up at four in the morning the day of an impending exam so I could study for a couple of hours. She had no alarm clock, so she stayed up, in order to wake me on time, only to watch me go back to sleep with the book on my chest. Still, before I took the bus to school, she said, "Get one hundred"—her way of telling me to do my best.

So, what to do now? I was told that one of my high school classmates had gone to the United States, enrolled in a city college, had part-time jobs, and needed minimal financial support from home. I thought I could do the same. It led to another choice of vocation: studying pharmacy, a reputable vocation in response to my parents' innocent expectations. I had the assumption that it was in line with chemistry. Even though it was another career I had no interest in and had little knowledge of, I believed it would be short-lived—an interim money-making vocation, a step toward attaining my goal.

Now that my mother knew of my plan to go abroad to study, she came to my bedroom one day and handed me a paper bag. In it I found the money I had given her during my two years as a medical representative. She had spent none of it. "Take it. It will pay for your school," she said.

I applied for admission to some universities and colleges

in the US and got accepted by a few in different states. I chose the University of New Mexico. I had a cousin in New York and a sister in California, but I didn't know anyone in New Mexico, so I felt my choice provided me freedom to no longer feel trapped doing what everyone else believed was the right thing for me to do.

What I knew of the United States was rudimentary. My impressions of the country and its peoples were from the popular American movies I had seen. They portrayed an exciting way of life in a faraway fantasy land. My brother had talked my father into turning his transportation business into a music shop, selling records and musical instruments. The few Americans in Amman who were embassy personnel often visited my brother's music shop to purchase classical records. Other than that, the Americans stayed on their own turf, unlike the British, who had more of a presence in the country and mingled with the locals, dining in their restaurants, eating falafel and hummus.

My brother enjoyed the Americans' visits, and they appreciated the service he provided. He'd offer them Turkish coffee, and they would linger, chatting about home acoustics and record players. Whenever I saw Americans at my brother's shop, I admired their friendliness and their casual and unpretentious demeanor. I thought I'd be happiest in America.

The substantial sum of money my mother handed me, and the possibility of working part-time while studying in the US, I was certain, would provide me with an education without having to rely on my parents' financial support.

My parents and brother assumed I would become a pharmacist, come back home, and open a pharmacy. But I had other ideas. My intention was to do the best I could to become a pharmacist, naively assuming that it would provide me with financial security to pursue my dream of becoming an artist. I'd given no thought to how long it would take or if it was at all possible.

The morning of my departure, I got up at five to join my parents who were seated on the veranda, having Turkish coffee. Their talk ceased when they saw me. Throughout the next hour or two, my mother was quiet. When I'd attended the university in Beirut and flew back and forth to spend vacations at home, she would say, "Watch out for pickpockets when riding the trams." With a three-inch safety pin, she would secure the inner pocket of my jacket where I kept my paper money. That morning, she offered none of that advice. She knew nothing of the country I was going to other than the occasional news she heard from my sister Alexandra about her life in the US. She and her husband had immigrated to California three years earlier, where Joseph worked as a waiter for George Mardikian's restaurant, Omar Khayyam, in San Francisco. My cousin Victor and his family had also immigrated to the US. Victor, who had been an electrician in Amman, had janitorial duties and a handyman job for an Armenian church in New York. He planned to meet me at the airport, and I would stay with him and his family for a day or two before proceeding to New Mexico.

CHAPTER 4

The Promise

On May 30, 1958, at 8 a.m. in Amman, my journey began. I was twenty-five years old and on my way to the United States to enroll in the school of pharmacy at the University of New Mexico in Albuquerque.

The night before I had been awake past midnight, torn by guilt. I had already blundered twice in my career choices, and I might be on the verge of doing it again. I had concealed my goal from my family, obsessed with a way of life I didn't quite understand and wouldn't expect my parents to. I knew that in the land where I was born and lived, art as a vocation was inconceivable.

Carrying my suitcase, I reached the moss-green iron gate of our home, my father by my side. Seeing the fragrant red honeysuckle my mother had planted many years before as a welcoming to guests, I paused for a moment. My eyes swept over our garden of rose bushes, ivy on the stucco wall, and rows of pansies and violets. It had been the sanctuary where I spent much time as a child dreaming of an imaginary world.

I set down my suitcase and looked back. My mother stood still by the veranda, framed by the pink and magenta bougainvillea vines that climbed the stone wall, reaching the flat roof. Her hands were clasped against her navy-blue-and-white polka-dot dress. I wanted to go and tell her that I would be back. But I couldn't. It would have been a promise I didn't intend to fulfill.

My mother came to embrace me. She placed her hands on my shoulders and looked straight in my eyes, an image I cannot erase from my mind. "I may never see you again," she said in Arabic.

Those were the last words I heard her speak, and they've haunted me ever since. I never saw my mother or my father again.

I boarded the plane, leaving my family and my home in the quest to fulfill my dream of being a different person experiencing a different life in a different world.

I closed my eyes and let my thoughts wander over my past and the uncertain future. I felt a tug on my arm. I opened my eyes. A boy no older than two smiled at me, oblivious to the strange environment. My thoughts went to a day in my very early childhood. I must have had a fever. My mother sponged my forehead with a cool wet rag while my father peered at me with anxiety and grave concern, for they had already experienced the loss of two sons, one stillborn and the other from illness. As my fever subsided, my mother and father must have sensed a sparkle in my eyes. Their faces lit up with loving smiles.

In my self-absorbed, restless existence that I believed uneventful and empty, I was leaving behind a comfortable life with a family who comforted me and supported me. My parents lived a simple life with selfless, unconditional love. Their lives focused on us, their sons and daughters—their endless responsibility. We burdened them with our problems and gave them nothing in return to assuage their worries and concerns, except that we were part of their lives as a family.

Strapped in my airplane seat, a choking loneliness swirled in my head, and I was unable to shake off that troublesome feeling weighing on my conscience, wrapped up in self-absorption, disregarding what my parents expected of me.

As the plane circled above the city, I looked out the window and there it was: the city of the desert, Amman. This would have been the hour when the city came alive. I pictured myself walking through the dusty streets among the native Arabs, as I had done most of my growing-up years.

When my parents married, my father was a driver for an Arab dignitary named Rekaby Pasha, whose office was in As-Salt, the capital of Transjordan. That's where my brother, Ohanness, was born. At the time of my birth, Amman had replaced As-Salt as the capital, and Rekaby's office had moved to Amman. It had then a few thousand dwellers. Amman became my parents' final destination.

On the Lufthansa plane, as we flew over Europe, Susan, an American journalist, sat next to me. She was a friendly and lively woman. She asked about my destination and my mission. Hearing of my ultimate intent to become an artist, she wondered why I had not enrolled in an art school instead of pharmacy. Then she agreed I would make good money in pharmacy, whereas it would be difficult to make a living in art—the troubling reality I already knew.

Over Germany, the plane had a minor problem and had to land in Frankfurt for repairs. We had the choice to either spend the night in Germany (with rooms and expenses provided and a car to drive us to the hotel in a small town close to Frankfurt) before continuing our flight the next day on the same plane, or to change planes immediately and proceed with our initial journey.

Susan opted to stay in Germany and so did I. (Since my cousin Victor who was to pick me up in New York knew of my itinerary, he would know of my delay.) Susan spoke German and was familiar with the small town where we spent the night. In the drive around the town, we came upon a rally, a heated gathering with a lot of shouting. Ever the journalist, Susan asked the driver to stop for a minute. She mingled with the Germans, asking questions, getting information on what was happening. I tagged along, fascinated by what was going on—an unhindered rally, unheard of where I came from.

On the plane the next day, she talked about life in the US—that it was a vast country with peoples of various national origins. Its people might seem self-absorbed, yet most would help when needed.

As I listened to her, she sensed my insecurity and anxiety. She welcomed me to stay for a day or two with her and some other friends in an apartment they rented in New York and said that she would show me the city and get me acclimated to the country. I thanked her and said that I expected my cousin to pick me up at the airport. I was awed but also intimidated by her assertive personality—something I had never seen in a woman before. I envied her extroversion. In contrast, I was timid, awkward, and clumsy when interacting with strangers.

I didn't sleep much in that small German town, and back on the plane, while passengers slept, including my friend, I remained wide awake throughout the flight across the ocean. All I could see out the small window was a never-ending darkness. I tried hard to concentrate on anything but what lay ahead for me, but failed. Whenever I faced up to the reality that I would be a student again and need to survive a year or two of drudgery, clueless as to where I was heading or what I was up against, the artistic future I envisioned seemed improbable and farfetched.

A bellowing voice on the intercom announced that we would soon be in New York. I felt a nudge, and my friend smiled widely at me. Through my window, New York seemed an endless city crammed with tall buildings. A chill came over me—excitement steeped in fear. What if cousin Victor wasn't there to meet me as planned?

The plane landed with a jolt and a roar, followed by an eerie quiet. Many stood and packed the aisle, as did Susan, who elbowed her way out of her seat. Apprehensive of what was to come, I stayed close to her. Off the plane, through a tunnel, I kept up with her quick pace, even though everyone else seemed to run past us. We were out into the terminal amid waves of people and deafening sounds. She turned to me, reminding me that I was welcome to stay with her and some other friends for a day or two. I thanked her and said I needed to wait for my cousin to pick me up. "Good luck," she said, and dashed away. People crisscrossed one another, and everyone seemed to be in a hurry—so many people crammed into one place, with deafening sounds and voices.

Over a loudspeaker, a woman seemed to be giving instructions. Unable to understand a word she was saying, I looked around at all the signs to direct me. None meant anything to me. I stood still for a few minutes, trying to make sense of this maze. *What if my cousin Victor doesn't show up? What should I do? Stay in one spot until he finds me?* I told myself not to panic. I saw an airline employee and asked him where I could get my luggage. He looked at my ticket stub with my flight number and, without a word, pointed in a general direction. I started walking. A man at the far end of the terminal, among a mass of people, waved. I watched him for a minute and then looked again—cousin Victor came to my rescue. It took me a while to fight my way through the crowd. I barely recognized him. Without a moustache, he had a withered face, unlike the handsome, rugged-looking Victor I remembered. He had lost weight and had a mellow disposition. He took charge and guided me to retrieve my luggage. Then we took a cab that drove for miles, at high speed.

The taxi stopped at an old three-story sooty building. Up the dimly lit, narrow stairs, we climbed to Victor's tiny apartment. When he unlocked the door, a distinct, savory aroma permeated the apartment. His wife, Haigouhi, had been preparing my favorite eggplant dish. Two young boys, who looked to be about six and eight years old, examined me with welcoming smiles.

Haigouhi came out of the cramped kitchen, dried her hands on her apron, and embraced me. "I bet you're hungry," she said. Of course I couldn't resist the alluring aroma of my favorite food. I said I wished she hadn't gone through all that trouble. "It's easy to prepare," she said.

Because of the large number of ethnic immigrants in that

part of New York, the variety of slender, lavender eggplant needed for the dish had been readily available. I remembered watching my mother scooping out the eggplant, then stuffing it with rice, ground meat, chopped onions, and parsley, seasoning it with black pepper and allspice, then stacking and cooking it in tomato sauce. We had the old-country stuffed eggplant meal with yogurt. Like many Armenians, Haigouhi took pride in her cooking creativity.

After supper, Victor mentioned that in the US, they associated wearing a moustache with shady characters or even gangsters. The boys giggled. Victor sensed my surprise. I had worn a moustache since I was in my teens—as soon as I was able to grow one.

That very evening, I shaved my moustache. Looking at my face in the mirror, I couldn't recognize myself. I thought I had lost my identity. The two boys stared at my face and snickered.

The boys wanted to surprise me. I followed them to a small room. In the corner was a TV—the first television I had ever seen. And in color! Back home for entertainment, we had an RCA radio. It sat in a bulky two-foot-high cabinet and had six-inch vacuum tubes, which we had to replace once a month, if not more frequently.

I was impressed by the TV, but not as much as by taking a shower and having water run over my face for as long as I wished. In Amman, we had had a water shortage for as long as I could remember. Throughout the day, my three sisters, my brother, and I, then finally my father and my mother, each took turns taking a bath. We sat on a low wooden stool in a claw-legged cast iron bathtub. The bathtub was on one side of our small bathroom. In front of us, on another stool, a small tub contained our ration of heated water. Water from an upright tank filled the tub. At 4 a.m. my mother burned wood in the compartment beneath the tank and maintained the fire throughout the day until the last one of us had taken a bath. Water tanks on the flat roof held a water supply sufficient for our weekly household needs, as well as filling the two barrels of water on each end of the house to irrigate our garden. Another impressive thing in the US was being able to use soft toilet paper and flush it down the toilet bowl instead of the thick paper we used back home, as thick as a manila envelope, that we placed in a can by the toilet and disposed of at the end of the day.

After the many sleepless hours since I had embarked on my journey, I finally had at least six hours of restful sleep. After a breakfast of fried white goat cheese, labneh balls (a thickened yogurt spread drizzled with olive oil), za'atar (a combination of spices, sumac, and toasted sesame seeds), and pita bread, Victor wanted to show me Manhattan. We took a cab. The gruff driver, a cigar in his mouth, drove amid a chaotic car jam, yet remained respectful of pedestrians and even, to a certain extent, other drivers, notwithstanding occasional cuss words or impatient gestures. It was unlike the crazy cab drivers in Amman (even worse than in Beirut). In Beirut I had seen drivers at high speed come to a stop just inches from a pedestrian—an intimidating practice.

We walked along congested sidewalks among people from many worlds. I was awed by the dazzling blue, red, and yellow blinking neon lights on enormous signs.

I followed Victor into a café. Young and old lined up to pick up their orders. Holding steaming hotdogs in long buns wrapped in paper, we proceeded to the condiment ledge. I watched Victor piling on his choices. I did the same.

One high point of my time in New York was our visit to the United Nations. Haigouhi's brother, who worked there, gave us a tour that included the empty assembly room.

The next morning, we took a cab to the Greyhound bus station. I bought a ticket. Destination: Albuquerque, New Mexico. After hugging my family goodbye, I boarded the bus. From then on, I was on my own, lost among strangers.

PART II

NEW MEXICO

CHAPTER 5

Back to School

My seat by the window behind the driver of the spacious Greyhound bus was a luxury—a far cry from my journeys between Amman and Jerusalem. As a young boy, I had no choice when picking a seat among the crowd of travelers, so I had to sit in the back seat of a taxi, sandwiched between two men, sometimes Bedouins, taking up more than their share of space with all the stuff they carried. Often the old taxi had torn-up seat covers and springs jutting through, padded by nauseating greasy sheep hide. The suffocating odor of sheep hide and sweat in the brutal environment would make me gag. I would tell myself to keep swallowing to avoid throwing up. Most times, somewhere around noon, close to Jericho, in an oppressive hot environment, the radiator would boil over. We would wait for minutes that seemed like an hour while the driver cooled the radiator by splashing cold water over the engine.

A woman with droopy eyes who looked like she had just gotten out of bed sat next to me on the Greyhound. The driver maneuvered the large bus around the narrow exit of the station. We swerved inches from the concrete walls while the engine murmured, interrupted by the occasional puffing sound of the brakes. Soon we were on the freeway, humming along at high speed. Towns large and small flashed by in a blur. At bus stops along the highways, some passengers disembarked, and others climbed on. In a small town, an elderly man pushing a boy in a wheelchair greeted the woman who had been seated next to me. She bent over the boy, showering him with kisses. Soon they were gone. A cheerful young man with a cowboy hat got on, patted the driver on the shoulder as if he knew him, then looked at me with a beaming smile like he knew me as well and took the vacant seat next to me. He wanted to know where I was heading. "Albuquerque," I said under my breath. He may not have heard me or understood what I said, or he may have realized I wasn't an interesting travel companion. He took a *Field & Stream* magazine from under his arm and turned page after page.

Throughout our travel, I got off the bus at the regular stops to have a cup of coffee or a pastry. As we drove west, the countryside transformed dramatically, as if we were in a different country. There were all kinds of people with various habits and ways of speaking, walking, and dressing. More men wore western Wrangler jeans than dress pants, donned wide belts with enormous shiny belt buckles, and wide-rimmed cowboy hats or baseball caps—quite unlike the fedoras men wore in New York. More women travelers wore Levi's jeans rather than skirts and had frizzy hair hanging over their shoulders. People appeared more casual and less hurried the farther west we traveled.

On the bus, I avoided talking to fellow travelers. Upon hearing my accent, they might have asked me where I came from, which would lead to lengthy small talk that I didn't want at the time.

After a couple of days of travel, in the dark, on the side of the road, I saw a sign that said "Las Vegas." The Las Vegas I had seen in a movie had flashy, brightly lit signs on nightclubs and gambling places. Here there was nothing, no cars in the narrow streets and no lights in the few homes that were barely visible.

It didn't take long before we were back on the freeway, speeding along. I soon realized we were in New Mexico, not Nevada. The countryside became drier, with no vegetation except for the tumbleweeds that flew across the highway—a terrain not unlike what one might see in some areas where I came from.

We arrived in Albuquerque sometime around 7 a.m. From the bus station, I took a taxi to the University of New Mexico. Having had little sleep throughout the bus trip, I was in a state of mental and physical exhaustion. My priority was finding the administration building so I could register for a place in one of the dorms.

As soon as I stepped on the campus grounds, my vision of the exciting new world vanished. Gripped with dismay, I walked over the gray sidewalks that might have been pitted by a sandstorm, not unlike the dusty grounds of downtown Amman. Massive adobe buildings, their makeup not much different from the adobe clay dwellings on hillsides and in valleys of Amman, were all I saw.

I was dismayed by the early morning emptiness around me, a scene devoid of life—not even a lone bird. The quietness of my surroundings evoked a state of loneliness and discontent. I wondered whether my reasoning to pick New

Mexico had merit, or if I should have picked California or New York with all the glitter that might have lifted my spirits and subdued my anxieties.

I sat on a bench and looked around. I knew I was in trouble, with no idea of what I was up against, lamenting all the days, the months, the years I had already wasted, searching blindly for a way of life that suited my temperament and promised me a happy life.

Close to the hour when the administration building opened and I could learn where I would live and what I would do next, a young man, the only person I had yet seen, approached me. He had dark eyes, thin black hair, a long angular face, jutting chin, and a swagger that projected confidence, yet he had a respectful and friendly demeanor. He greeted me with a broad, sincere smile and introduced himself. "I'm Robert Ghattas," he said. He didn't seem to be the typical American that I had seen so far. With an overly stressed, drawling American accent, he said he was Lebanese, from Beirut. His family still lived there, and he had graduated with a degree in chemistry here at UNM. When I mentioned my name, he asked where I was from. He was surprised and delighted when he found out that I had studied at AUB and that I, too, had a degree in chemistry.

"So, why are you . . . ?" his voice trailed, his eyes shifting toward the administration building.

I told him I was about to enroll in the pharmacy school. "That's a great idea. I think I'll do the same," he said. I suspected it wasn't a notion that he had already contemplated.

The adobe buildings on the campus didn't look that bad

after all. My initial disappointment dissipated with Robert's appearance, especially after I learned that the adobe-style structures reflected the American Indian culture.

The administration assigned me a dorm room, and I scheduled a meeting with Dean Cataline of the school of pharmacy for consultation. The dean, a gracious man, informed me, to my dismay, that the school of pharmacy would accept AUB's chemistry curriculum, but to become a registered pharmacist, I needed to attend three full years in the school of pharmacy and a one-year program of mandatory internship—six months interning in a pharmacy before graduation and another six months after graduation. This new revelation was most troubling, and I had no clue how to respond.

Now I faced a dismaying situation I dreaded. I'd be a student for more years than I'd expected. More disconcerting was the expense I'd incur without reaching out for help from my father. I hadn't told my parents my desire to become an artist. Some members of my family had seen some of my small sketches and given me compliments, yet in their minds, it seemed to be a passing hobby that had no intrinsic value, similar to my brother's stamp collecting hobby. To have art as a vocation would be an absurd proposition.

Facing Dean Cataline's revelation, I had to respond. "I'd like to enroll in summer school to shorten my years of enrollment," I said.

"It would be a very heavy load with daylong lab work, and I wouldn't recommend it."

"I can do it if you'd only let me take the challenge."

The summer program was quite demanding. All day long,

I was in the lab in a pharmacology class or in the field along the Rio Grande collecting samples for microscopic study in zoology class.

I was a diligent student, paid attention in class, and had top grades, which made me eligible for a small scholarship. But the scholarship and the money my mother had given back to me weren't enough to meet my expenses in the US and relieve me of the financial difficulty I was in. As frugal as I was, the cost of my day's meals equaled what my family spent weekly on food. I could no longer justify living in the dorm. Robert and I rented a small, rundown apartment close to campus. We painted the two bedrooms, the living room, the small kitchen, and the bathroom and turned it into a comfortable apartment. And more importantly, I was able to prepare my own sandwiches rather than have lunches in the cafeteria.

I had three part-time jobs: washing orange juice bottles at a small-scale operation near our apartment, cleaning rat and mice cages at the pharmacy department lab, and janitorial work on campus.

In my juice bottle–washing job, I worked alone. They paid me seventy-five cents an hour. Over a horizontal, motorized rotating brush submerged in soapy water and Clorox, I held each bottle with dried up juice. If the phone rang, I had to dry my hands quickly and take orders in that noisy place. By the time I finished a couple of hours' work, my hands were raw. Walking to our apartment, noises, real or imaginary, buzzed in my ears.

For my second job, it might sound childish, but the sight of a mouse, rat, or slithering snake, even at a distance, made me uneasy. In our pharmacy lab, we learned how to restrain rats. As squeamish as I was, I had to get used to handling white rats and mice, a prerogative in our lab course.

Rats and mice cage–cleaning without guidance was a disconcerting job. It also paid me seventy-five cents an hour. Every Friday evening, filled with dread anticipating the unnerving quiet hour, I would enter the dimly lit lab. The cages were lined on benches. The musty odor of the rodents permeated the room and was even more pronounced than in daylight hours. The pink eyes of every rat and mouse seemed to focus on me as I approached the cages.

To clean the soiled cages, I had to move the rodents, one by one, to cages that were clean with fresh bedding. Salty sweat would run down my forehead and over my eyes in rivulets. Distracting and restraining a rat with babies wasn't easy. The protective mother would strike the cage as soon as my hand approached the wire.

I would sit for minutes, assessing the situation and trying to muster courage. The pharmacology professor who hired me had told me not to worry. "They're clean of diseases," he said. He meant I shouldn't worry if I got bitten, which wasn't reassuring in the slightest.

Most of my janitorial work was done in the various departments on campus. It amounted to cleaning toilets, mopping bathrooms, sweeping floors, dusting, and picking up trash from offices and classrooms. I looked forward to cleaning in the art department. While emptying trash cans, I would linger and smell the wonderful scent of turpentine and oil paint. For me, it was a seductive perfume. Large, dazzling abstract paintings by students and faculty instructors leaned along the perimeter of the walls and a few on huge easels. Sometimes, looking at the large abstract paintings on a few of the easels, I would have the urge to scoop up a juicy glob of oil paint and apply it to the canvas. Many years later, I learned that the well-known artist Richard Diebenkorn may have been a faculty member at the University of New Mexico during my enrollment. I did not know who he was at the time and was not familiar with his abstract style of work. The paintings I saw in classrooms might have been his.

Occasionally, janitorial work required physical exertion, such as waxing and buffing the wooden athletic courts. I worked with a couple of full-time, seasoned Mexican janitors. The head janitor told me to buff using the three-foot diameter powerful electric buffer. He and his assistant stood around rolling cigarettes, watching me. When I turned on the buffer, it took off, dragging me along with it. I tried to muscle it, but it was futile. They laughed at my predicament and my struggle. Then one of the two came to my rescue. With his fingers lightly touching the handle, it purred, tame as a kitten, sliding over and caressing the floor. "It's all in balance and light touch," he said with an air of haughtiness.

Soon I enjoyed their company. One of them said I would make a good husband for his niece, and he welcomed me to meet his family. I wasn't sure if he had said it in jest or really meant it. I told him I already had a girlfriend.

CHAPTER 6

Speech Class

At the University of New Mexico, a prerequisite for graduation for all students, in all departments, including pharmacy, was a speech class. Being an introvert and a foreigner with an accent, it was the class I dreaded most. For me, talking to strangers, whether one person or a group, was extremely stressful.

In the class, one by one we faced classmates enrolled in various departments and gave a five-minute speech about a subject of our choice. We were expected to elicit their interest and gain their attention. It brought to mind the unnerving two years I spent as a medical representative in Amman, agonizing over every encounter. In that situation, I dealt with one person at a time, a physician whom I needed to talk to convincingly about our product. Here I faced a group of students, all strangers.

In my presentation, I showed how to culture a petri dish, as done in the pharmacy lab. In the nutrient mass in the dish, I incised zigzagged lines with a fine needle that in the lab would have had live bacteria on its tip. After I illustrated the process, I pulled out an already cultured dish, showing the growth of the bacteria over the previously incised lines in the medium.

On the first day of class, a young woman chose the seat next to me. Since we both had a habit of going to class early, we sat next to each other throughout the course and always managed to strike up a conversation. It would have been unnerving for me to approach a girl or a woman and converse. In Amman, the only relationship a young man could have had with a woman was to be engaged or married. Most women or girls I knew were my relatives.

This young woman's vivacious personality, candor, and sincerity made it easy for me to open up and respond to her inquiries. What was the origin of my unusual name? What was I majoring in? Where did I grow up?

She told me her name was Karen Albach. She talked about herself, her father, and her brother. Her mom passed on when Karen was sixteen years old, and they lived in Santa Fe, New Mexico. A lovely town, she said.

It wasn't long before we talked freely as friends. Despite my introversion, I was eager to talk to her about myself: about the origin of my surname, my solitary childhood life, and, although I was enrolled in pharmacy, my dream to someday become an artist—an aspiration I hadn't divulged to anyone, even to my friend Robert. With her, I felt comfortable revealing my goal.

One of us, and I believe it was her, suggested we go have a cup of coffee somewhere, sometime.

"Would tomorrow be okay?" I blurted out with a forwardness not in my nature. I knew I had free time after my janitorial work.

"Yes, that'd be good."

That's how it began—a sincere friendship with no complexity, no discomfort.

Apart from the young men I knew and roomed with,

three Middle Easterners and one from Mexico City, I had no time to befriend anyone else. My three part-time jobs, and my full-time enrollment in the school of pharmacy left little time to socialize with others, not even with my roommates. But Karen was different. Throughout my life, I yearned for genuine female companionship, and she was the catalyst to make it possible. And that set the course of our togetherness.

We sat in a café with a twenty-five-cent tub of french fries and talked. On some weekends, we spent time at the zoo. At the music building, I listened to her practice piano. My financial problems did not affect our friendship, except for limiting the time and the quality of our being together.

My foreign upbringing placed no undesirable stress on our friendship. It seemed to augment her interest in me. I was at ease in her presence and didn't feel the need to impress her. As the weeks passed, we developed a dependency on each other, a bond grounded in personal need for one another beyond casual friendship.

In my junior year, I started work mopping floors and stocking shelves at a pharmacy in Albuquerque. Late one evening, early in my employment, my boss asked me to deliver a prescription. I had just learned how to drive and gotten my driver's license. His huge American station wagon had power steering and power brakes which, in those days, were extremely sensitive. The car swerved as soon as I touched the steering wheel. I weaved through unfamiliar side roads like a drunk driver. A touch on the brake evoked a jarring response. Reading house numbers in the dimly lit evening while driving that monstrosity of a car was an impossible feat. Cars behind me kept honking their horns, adding to my befuddlement. I went round and round the neighborhood blocks. When I saw a headlight beaming in my direction, I pulled over, jumping the curb.

Somehow, I found the house and delivered the prescription. But on my way back, I ran out of gas. I couldn't call my boss. What could he do? It was his only car.

I walked for a few blocks to a phone booth and called Karen, who had a car. She drove me to a gas station, where I bought a gas can and a gallon of gas. When I walked into the drugstore, the look my boss gave me impressed on me that he didn't want to hear my sad story. Not being able to do deliveries, I would be useless. I quit my job.

I found an evening job at a large chain drugstore. The manager said I was scheduled to work at the pharmacy from 6 to 9 p.m. for five dollars an hour—a lot more than I made at my other jobs. When I showed up to work, the manager and the pharmacist on duty left the store, leaving me alone in a predicament. I had no clue what they expected of me. The non-pharmacist manager either didn't know the law, or he did and purposefully didn't ask for my credentials. I was an intern expected to work in the pharmacy under the supervision of a registered pharmacist.

A man handed me a prescription vial he wanted refilled. I explained my situation and convinced him to leave it and the pharmacist would fill it in the morning. He said that was fine; he wasn't in a hurry to have the medicine. Then a woman handed me a new prescription. When I tried to explain the situation to her, she snatched the paper out of my hand and left.

That evening, I told Robert of my experience. "You're lucky you aren't in jail," he said. That job was also short-lived.

At some point, I asked my father for some financial help to finish my studies. For a few months, he was able to relieve me of my dire money woes. What he sent me and what I earned from my part-time jobs was sufficient to pay our landlord. My father had done a lot for me in the past, more than I expected or deserved. It was troubling for me to think about his support while I earned my chemistry degree, which had turned out to be fruitless.

At the end of my junior year, I faced a dilemma. My father would no longer be able to assist me financially. The scholarship and part-time jobs weren't enough to meet my essential expenses and without some financial help from home, I wouldn't be able to complete my senior year and graduate. And again, I would be a total failure.

Dean Cataline, aware of my desperate situation, recommended me for summer apprenticeship work at Dragon Drugs in Los Alamos. He assumed my wages, along with my small scholarship, might meet my senior year financial obligations. Nevertheless, I knew that the two months' wages working at the drugstore wouldn't be sufficient to pay for tuition, room, and board. Yet it would fulfill my pre-graduation internship requirement, so I went along with a naive hope for a miracle.

Los Alamos, to a certain extent, was still a restricted town due to the Manhattan Project. I rented a one-room apartment with a kitchenette from the US government. I borrowed one of Karen's family's camping beds—an army cot with a foldable canvassed wooden frame as well as a thin mattress and a pillow. Karen visited me on weekends, bringing a can of muffin dough that we baked and snacked on with slices of gouda cheese.

Working at a drugstore as a pharmacy student intern meant getting familiarized with the pharmacy practice. But that didn't happen. My work at Dragon Drugs was sweeping floors and stocking shelves. The pharmacy manager, a temperamental man who wasn't the owner of the drugstore, dictated my work status and wouldn't let me set foot in the pharmacy. "You would be in my way," he said.

Once in a while, on weekdays, the drugstore owner, Bob Dragon, visited the store. He was a taciturn man who didn't even greet any of his employees in passing. The atmosphere for all of us always changed with his unexpected appearances. Even the grumpy pharmacist became congenial. Mr. Dragon spent most of his time in the office, conferring with the bookkeeper who worked a few hours a week and stayed in her office. Yet he made it a practice to come out and walk the aisles with a pad in his hand, surveying the shelves and taking notes.

By the end of summer, I was resigned to the idea that it was impossible to finish the last year of my studies. My job at Dragon Drugs would end, and my dire financial situation hadn't changed. I had no viable solution to my predicament. Without a degree and a license to practice pharmacy in the US, I'd have limited low-paying job possibilities, and the financial independence that I counted on (or hoped for) to attain my goal of becoming an artist would vanish.

I had convinced my family that if I studied pharmacy at a US university, I wouldn't be a burden on them for long.

Of course, that didn't happen, at least not immediately. And I was haunted by and couldn't shake the guilt from my ulterior motive.

In desperation, I decided I'd try the impossible. Everyone at the drugstore, including the pharmacist, considered Mr. Dragon a tough man to bargain with. I asked the pharmacist if it was possible that Mr. Dragon might loan me the money to complete my studies. His response was a bout of hilarious laughter, like he had heard the funniest joke ever.

"You must be crazy," he said. "Bob Dragon wouldn't loan his own sons a dime, let alone you."

He had known him much longer than I had. He had been working for him for eight years. I had only been there seven weeks.

In one of his Friday visits, Mr. Dragon walked the aisles as usual, taking notes. I was mopping the floor up and down the aisles.

When I caught up with his long strides, I said, "Mr. Dragon . . ." He turned around and gave me a look, but continued walking.

"I won't be able to pay for my senior year," I said.

I thought he hadn't heard me.

"If you'd loan me the money to complete my senior year, I promise I'll pay you back."

He hesitated for a moment, turned his back to me, then scribbled something on his notepad and walked away without saying a word.

It was a huge mistake. *I shouldn't have done that,* I thought. Why would anyone give me, a foreigner without a legitimate address, a loan? Glumly, I resumed my mopping, resigned to the thoughts going through my mind.

"Sarkis, come to the office." The secretary's voice boomed on the intercom. I had never talked to the secretary except for casual greetings.

I screwed up this time for sure, I thought. *I'm fired.* It would be a major embarrassment to explain my stupidity to the dean who had recommended me for the job.

I placed the mop in the broom closet and went to the office. By that time, Mr. Dragon had left.

"Mr. Dragon said you needed a loan to complete your senior year," she said. "What do you have in mind?"

I thought I would faint. She didn't seem upset or combative, and I couldn't believe her mellow vibe.

"Two hundred dollars a month would pay my expenses," I said.

She wrote something on a piece of paper and slid it toward me.

"Sign here," she said.

I looked at the brief note. It said something like, "I will pay Mr. Bob Dragon of Dragon Drugs what I owe him." It had no deadline or mention of interest or other pertinent information. In a state of disbelief, I scribbled my signature.

On the first of each month of my senior year, I received a check for two hundred dollars.

CHAPTER 7

Farmington

L ove at first sight, physical infatuation, or blind admiration weren't what brought Karen and me together. In our relationship, mutually unselfish caring, unconditional acceptance of one another, and giving each other solace provided a strong desire for a lifelong, permanent companionship—marriage.

When we announced our decision to our families, we faced negative responses, but for different reasons. Karen's father wanted her to marry someone from his church and not a foreigner. My family knew that once I married, the chances I would go back home would be nil. Although the responses we got were unfortunate, they had no effect on our commitment.

On June 7, 1961, Karen and I graduated, she with a BFA in music and a minor in elementary education, and I with a BS in pharmacy. We married and headed to Farmington, New Mexico, where we both found employment. Karen taught second grade, and I was a full-time pharmacy intern at William Drugs. I'd be fulfilling my after-graduation six months internship required for pharmacist registration.

For many young married couples, the honeymoon period is magical. For us, it meant facing problems right from the start. We rented a one-room furnished apartment. Soon we found out it was cockroach-infested. When we turned on the light in the bathroom, they scurried in all directions—on the floor, walls, and ceiling. Finding a centipede under the covers of our bed the first night caused sleepless hours as we considered ways to make the apartment livable. During the next few days, we painted the walls, fumigated the bathroom, scrubbed and sterilized the kitchen counters, and sealed most of the windows.

My pharmacy studies behind me, and now with full-time employment, I hoped the problems that plagued me would vanish. But beginning a new life wasn't easy. I found myself on a demanding journey, immersing myself in the American way of life. At UNM, foreign students congregated around one another. The young men I knew, or roomed with, were foreigners—one from Syria, one from Jordan, Robert from Lebanon, and my first roommate at the dorm was from Mexico City. Karen adapted to my foreignness more than I took the effort to adapt to her American attributes. She wasn't the type to flaunt her Americanism. She didn't even correct my pronunciation or my muddled sentences. I had a good grasp of the English language despite having a foreign accent. Looking back, I wish I had taken the time to improve my speech and try to lessen or eliminate my foreign accent. I would have been a much happier American.

Once we had our apartment livable, I walked to Williams Drugs to meet and introduce myself to Bill Williams, the owner.

Bill, a charming man in his forties, welcomed me with a sincere smile and a hearty handshake that put me at ease. A woman in her sixties sat on a stool, tending to a prescription file. As soon as I stepped behind the counter, she stood and approached me. She had black hair, black eyes, and wore a flowery blouse and a long black skirt. She offered her hand.

"Welcome, Sarkis."

"This is Ada," Bill said. "We can't do without her."

Bill acquainted me superficially with the setup of the pharmacy and gave me the keys to the store. I had one week to get settled before starting my work schedule.

I soon found out I was in a quandary. I wasn't an intern supervised by a registered pharmacist complying with the New Mexico Board of Pharmacy's requirement for internship. I was the sole pharmacist on duty, taking on the responsibility of a licensed pharmacist, breaking the law right from the start of my career.

I didn't have any idea what retail pharmacy entailed. In our senior year, our professor skimmed over the retail pharmacy practice, although most pharmacy students went into retail pharmacy, not its alternatives, like hospital pharmacy, teaching, or research. I doubt that he himself had ever worked in a retail pharmacy.

The six-month pre-graduation internship and the six-month internship after graduation, stipulated by the New Mexico Board of Pharmacy, required the pharmacy intern to gain familiarity with the retail operation while supervised by a registered pharmacist. The interns were to gain experience in receiving phoned-in prescriptions, reading physicians' written prescriptions, and adhering to the law in refilling prescriptions, especially pertaining to dispensing scheduled medications, such as amphetamines and other addictive drugs. When filling a new prescription, interns were to gain experience in providing person-to-person guidance to the patient concerning the medication—clarifying side effects, stating correct usage, and so on. In my pre-graduation internship at Dragon Drugs, that hadn't happened.

In the school of pharmacy, we had learned the generic names of the drugs. We weren't familiar with the brand names that were on the shelves of the pharmacy. I should have experienced that as well during my time at Dragon Drugs.

On my first day at the pharmacy counter, Bill Williams was nowhere to be found. A woman in her sixties handed Ada a new prescription, and Ada gave it to me.

"Where is Bill?" the customer snapped.

"Bill took a day off. Sarkis is our new pharmacist, and we are delighted to have him."

The woman didn't respond. Her eyes shifted back to me. She stood at the cash register, glaring at me.

At most pharmacies, including Williams Drugs, tablets and capsules on shelves are in alphabetical order in a U-shaped compartment, the liquids in a separate compartment, and the scheduled drugs in a locked cabinet. I laid the prescription on the counter and kept telling myself to concentrate and show confidence. I needed to find the pills on the unfamiliar shelves. The woman's eyes followed every move I made while I searched for the prescribed medicine. She ignored Ada, who tried to distract her by small talk.

After finding the medication, I walked to the checkout counter, holding the prescription vial. It was my first experience dealing with a patient face-to-face. Ada moved to the side, allowing me to take her space. The woman eyed the vial in my hand.

With a smile, I said, "Mrs. Jones, these capsules could make you drowsy, and . . ." She had a puzzled look, as if straining to figure out what I was saying. That made me anxious. I repeated myself, rephrasing my words and speaking slower and more deliberately, continuing my instructions.

I thanked her and placed the vial on the counter. She didn't respond. Instead, she picked up the vial and kept turning it over and over, then placed it on the counter.

While Ada waited on Mrs. Jones, the phone rang, and I answered it. "Let me talk to Bill," a woman said in a sharp and impatient voice.

"Bill is off today, may I . . ."

"Let me talk to the pharmacist," she interrupted.

"Speaking."

There was a few moments' pause, then, catching me off guard, she rattled off a prescription without telling me she was a nurse. I prayed to heaven that I didn't need to call her back to verify what she had said.

I chose pharmacy without knowing what the profession was all about. I realized that all the courses of pharmacology, biochemistry, pharmacognosy, and hours of lab work were aimed at educating pharmacy students on the effect of drugs on the human body. They provided general education to improve students' knowledge of healthcare and also their ability to find answers to questions in reference books when needed. The teaching did not focus on the primary requirement of retail pharmacy, the branch of pharmacy practice that most pharmacy students choose. Retail pharmacy not only entails dispensing prescribed medications that physicians order, but also building the trust essential in the relationships with patients and being supportive of their well-being.

Ada proved indispensable. She knew the location of the drugs since she was the one who stocked the shelves when we received orders from the wholesalers. And she knew most of the local customers. She answered phone calls and engaged customers who waited for their prescriptions.

It didn't take long for me to befriend local customers, doctors, and nurses, and I finally felt at ease. Whenever I wasn't busy filling prescriptions, in many ways I enjoyed people's company.

Nevertheless, my internship at Williams Drugs was an experience in lack of professionalism. We didn't even have a tray and a spatula to count pills. Instead, we counted them by hand, one at a time, disregarding hygienic issues. Most importantly, I was never supervised by a registered pharmacist. I broke the law for six months doing the work of a registered pharmacist. Bill was behind the pharmacy counter only when I had a day off, which was once a week. Whenever he was at the store, he was on the floor talking with customers. Ada was my savior.

In the months I worked in Farmington, I finally fulfilled my six-month after-graduation internship requirement and became a registered pharmacist in the state of New Mexico. Karen and I also gained some financial security and paid off my last loan payment to Bob Dragon.

For a while, Karen drove our car and I walked to work. Now that we had achieved some financial security, we bought a beautiful, almost fluorescent-blue VW Bug. When I drove on the highway, the driver of another Bug coming in my direction, a kindred spirit, would flash his or her headlights to tell me, "Hey, my friend, I have one of those too." Those were the years when there was some camaraderie on the highway. And those were the times I gave hitchhikers, men or women, rides with no concern whatsoever.

It pleased me when Karen's father eventually accepted me as his son-in-law and seemed proud of me. Not long after we made our first apartment livable, he offered us a piano, dining room table, chairs, and cabinet. We bought a bed and moved into a new apartment.

Eventually, Bill hired a part-time pharmacist, Cal, to fill in on my days off and take the evening shift. Our work overlapped for an hour, and I enjoyed working with him. Cal was a pleasant, clean-cut guy, around seventy years old, who didn't keep it secret that he was in AA. Whenever he had the chance, he talked about his alcohol addiction he said had ruined his life. He did little favors for everyone, including me, buying me soft drinks, insisting as much as I objected.

Within a couple of months of being hired, he asked Bill for a week's vacation. He needed to visit his relatives in California. At the end of the week he phoned, asking for an extension of his vacation for one more week.

When he returned, he was a different person altogether. I could have sworn I had never seen the man in my life. He had the look of a derelict—puffy eyes, cuts on his forehead, bare feet caked with grime, gashes on his ankles and hands, shirt and trousers torn, and he reeked. It was a sad apparition.

He pushed his way behind the pharmacy counter and

demanded money. When I tried to talk him into leaving the building, he became belligerent. A customer called the cops, and they hauled Cal away. Ada phoned AA and told them his whereabouts. It saddened me to see him in that abject state. I still think of him, sober and at his best, a pleasant man, clean-shaven in a white shirt and a navy-blue tie.

In time, I became aware that our pharmacy had broken the strict drug law concerning frequency of dispensing amphetamines. The law had stringent restrictions on dispensing amphetamines and narcotics and identified them as "scheduled drugs." Pharmacists couldn't refill such drugs, and physicians couldn't phone in prescriptions; they had to be written and filed in separate files. The pharmacists and the physicians shared the responsibility of adhering to the law, including the frequency in dispensing such drugs.

The Federal Bureau of Narcotics got wind of the violation in dispensing those drugs. Early one morning, they took over the pharmacy and ordered us out, and throughout the day, they went through the restricted drug prescription files and inventory. Luckily, I wasn't implicated since I hadn't filled any of those prescriptions.

Soon after, Williams Drugs shut down and, through a recommendation from the wholesale drug company, McKesson, I found employment working for Ira Cato of Cato Drugs in Gallup, New Mexico, where Karen was hired to teach second grade.

I have fond memories of Farmington and its people who had a small-town, uncomplicated, and relaxed way of life. Most men loved to fish, and their conversation centered around fishing, so I, too, took up the hobby. It wasn't as much about catching fish as it was about conversing with the men on the subject. I wanted to belong to a community with similar values and interests. I bought my first rod and reel and accompanied local men night-fishing for catfish. Sitting on a stool with young and old enthusiasts on a cool moonlit night was the relief from pharmacy work that I needed.

Most memorable for me was fishing in the Colorado streams across the state line from Farmington. With fishing rod and reel, I learned to wade through the sparkling shallow streams. Out in nature, I imagined that someday I would become a painter and walk in the footsteps of the Impressionists, roaming the countryside. Instead of a rod and reel, I would carry my easel and canvas and paint the lovely landscape wherever I was.

CHAPTER 8

Gallup

Having already had a tumultuous year in the retail pharmacy practice, I entered Cato Drugs and walked to the pharmacy to introduce myself. Ira Cato, in a white smock, stood behind the prescription counter, talking to an older woman.

As I approached the pharmacy, his attention turned to me. The night before, I had planned my introduction. Yet face-to-face with Cato, I didn't have much to say. He had an overpowering posture and seemed gruff, with a raspy, deep voice. He stepped down from behind the counter with a smile and did all the talking, making it clear he was glad to see me. He introduced me to the two clerks on the floor and to his mother behind the pharmacy counter, who did his bookkeeping. When he greeted a customer passing by, he introduced me as his new pharmacist.

Within a week, Cato handed me the keys to the store and trusted me as his manager, and from then on, I was the sole pharmacist on duty. Cato showed up only to deal with major decision-making situations in the business's operation or to talk to his mother.

I worked long hours almost every day of the week, and often the police chief, a friend of Cato's, would call me in the middle of the night to open the pharmacy and fill a prescription needed in an emergency situation. I would put on a coat over my pajamas and drive down. Over the four years I worked for Cato, he totally relied on me, and my work ethic never disappointed him.

At first glance, Gallup looks like a dull town set in a gray-and-tan flat landscape with shallow hillsides and occasional rocky terrain. It's how I envision the landscape of the moon. Some tumbleweeds and sagebrush showcased its vast, otherwise barren landscape.

Set along old Route 66, Gallup was a tourist town. With its large Navajo population, it had, at the time, a "cowboys and Indians" reputation. Shops sold Indigenous American artifacts, pottery, and jewelry. Its only artistic flavor was during the yearly Gallup Inter-Tribal Indian Ceremonial, when many tribes from across the Americas converged onto the town to perform their colorful dances. It was especially enjoyable to watch the Aztec men dancing on a small platform atop a very tall pole. Many who came to the store to shop for incidentals didn't look like the Navajo tribe of Gallup or the Mexicans of Albuquerque, either. They were very tall and slim with large black eyes.

Whether the local men were real cowboys or not, most looked the part, wearing cowboy boots, cowboy hats, western shirts, Levi's jeans, and leather belts with silver buckles. I wanted to be a member of the local community of men, so I also wore western clothing.

In small towns such as Gallup and Farmington, hunting, fishing, and spending time outdoors in nature had a profound place in people's way of life. On occasion, men came to the store without their wives to refill their family prescriptions. They passed time visiting with friends, telling fishing and hunting stories, or lingering at the magazine rack reading Field & Stream articles and admiring the fishing tackle and gun photos. Because pharmacy business in the evenings was slow, they felt comfortable chatting with me and offered their expertise and know-how pertaining to guns and fishing and hunting in the surrounding areas. Although for me killing wildlife was inconceivable, I valued and pursued the skills essential in these sports.

In Gallup most men were gun owners. My fascination with guns was rekindled. I had always been fond of the pellet gun my father bought me when I was twelve years old. He made sure I knew it was not a toy, and said that any bird I shot, I would have to eat. Target shooting fascinated me; shooting a moving target was a challenge. The only moving target we had were the sparrows, so I hunted sparrows. When I shot ten or more, I would clean and fry them. My father and I would have them for dinner. We ate the tender sparrow meat and bones. He savored them with his nightly arak and made a big show of their delicacy, most likely for my benefit.

Unlike hunting sparrows, hunting deer was a serious matter that fascinated me, not for the killing but for the skill involved in tracking. Knowing that with some knowledge of guns and fishing tackle, I could converse with the local men on hunting and fishing, I bought a .30-30 Winchester rifle. It was the type that cowboys carried in the Louis L'Amour books I read. Its unique shape made it the preferred rifle for horsemen since it fit in a rifle holster on the side of a saddle.

I bought it for its historical appeal. I also bought a .30-06, fitted with a scope that a customer recommended. I used it for target practice.

Tracking wildlife in the forest had an appeal I couldn't resist. A local hunter told me that the best chance of seeing deer was to be in the woods before daybreak when the deer would be on the move. Since I had never seen deer in real life before, I was intrigued. Following his suggestion, before daybreak I drove to a wooded area and parked my pickup and started walking. Even with moonlight, walking in the darkness of the woods, hearing the cracking of twigs or snapping of limbs was eerie. Aware of creeping shadows of shapes imagined or real, I had the unsettling feeling that I wasn't alone, not unlike an experience I remembered from my childhood.

On a blustery night when I was around eight years old, my father asked me to go outside and shut the slatted shutters to the bedroom that was at the far end of our house. In the pitch dark, I sensed shrieking voices in my ears with every step I took. I felt as though someone or something was right behind me. Every few steps, as if in defiance, I'd halt for a few seconds. With my eyes closed, I cringed, expecting the worst. The closer I got to the shutters, the more their pounding against the stone wall quickened and magnified. I shuddered with fear. I hurried on my way back, my steps turning into a run, and once back in the blinding light of our home, I was at peace.

Now as an adult, I again had the unsettling feeling that I wasn't alone. I was startled to see a couple of hunters walking in my direction as the darkness lifted. I immediately retreated to my pickup. Thinking back to that morning, I wonder what wild animals, unseen, may have lurked in the bushes watching me.

A friend, John Bubany, bragged about his hunting experience and suggested we go hunting together. He was a very likable guy and easy to talk to—a man who I believed would be an excellent companion on an outdoor excursion. We planned a three-day hunting trip to a location he knew.

For the two nights of the hunt, we planned to sleep in the camper I had built of plywood and two-by-fours to fit my pickup. We packed our sleeping bags, some canned ham and beans, corned beef, and other food items he suggested. I took my new .30-06 rifle. John had his old army open-sight rifle.

He drove my pickup and talked of his hunting experiences throughout our drive. At high elevation, we encountered deep snow. At some point, he took a side road and parked in a spot not too far from the highway.

We decided to scout the area. We walked through dense trees and brush, looking for fresh deer droppings and tracks. After about an hour of trudging, we came upon what seemed to have been a meadow that was now covered with a foot of snow. Three does and a buck emerged from the distant dense woods, walking in our direction. If the deer had seen us, they showed no alarm.

My heart pounded with anticipation, hoping that the next morning, the first day of the hunting season, we would see them again. We retreated, following our tracks to the pickup.

We picked up some semi-dry twigs and branches, and John started a fire. He brewed coffee, and we sat on stools by the fire, talking about the following morning's expected hunt with a certainty of spotting that group of deer.

We were up before daybreak, only to find our boots frozen as hard as rocks. John started a fire with some twigs and branches that we had stored under the pickup. We placed our frozen boots in the fire to thaw and watched them steam up. He added fresh coffee to the grounds of the coffee from the previous evening. He said, "That's cowboy coffee—never throw out the grounds, just add fresh coffee."

Over dry, thick socks, our boots were still wet but thawed. We had snack bars to munch on—there was no time for a proper breakfast. We were on our way with rifles loaded and held against our shoulders like veteran hunters. Instead of the quiet of the previous day, our steps crunched loudly over the frozen layers of snow.

We arrived at the promising spot we had discovered the day before and stood waiting with overwhelming anticipation. The morning light glistened over the surface of the ice. An hour passed, then two hours. Holding my breath to prevent the freezing cold entering my lungs, I looked at John's face. His teeth were chattering, his nose was running, his cheeks were almost crimson. He glanced at me. "Let's get the hell out of here," he said.

As soon as he said those words, we heard crashing sounds in the distance. We froze, then saw a couple of guys in orange vests walking in our direction. They said they had scouted the area, and like us, had given up.

By the time it was midmorning the sun shone and at camp we had a cup of cowboy coffee and a candy bar and walked in different directions, hoping we might sight deer. But they were nowhere. There was not even evidence of fresh tracks.

John pulled out a pouch of Beech-Nut tobacco and gave me some to chew. He said it was the best remedy to keep us from getting thirsty. By now we were sweaty and tired from treading the packed snow with our heavy, wet boots. We kept on chewing and spitting the brown tobacco, staining the pristine snow.

By noon, we were back at the pickup. We lit a fire and warmed up some ham and beans and made some more cowboy coffee. We brought out a bottle of whiskey and sipped on it for warmth.

The walk in the afternoon was just about the same with no deer in sight, and again we saw a few hunters who had had no luck either. We didn't even hear shots, near or far. The third day, ready to go home, John tacked a piece of paper on a huge dead fir trunk, wanting to try his rifle that he hadn't shot for years. It turned out that his old, almost antique, army rifle was more accurate and much more comfortable to shoot than my fancy scoped .30-06 Winchester. Come to think of it, as much as I enjoyed being outdoors with my friend, not having to shoot at deer was a relief.

My boss, Cato, enjoyed dove hunting. He asked me to accompany him and a friend on a dove hunting trip. I bought a single-barreled 20-gauge shotgun for that hunt, while he and his friend had double-barreled 12-gauge shotguns. I rode with Cato in his pickup while his friend followed us in his car. Before daybreak, we were at the hunt site. We expected doves to fly to a huge cattle water tank around fifty yards in the distance. Cato brought out three cans of Vienna sausages and three cans of beer, and that was our breakfast.

In the sport of dove hunting, we were to shoot at birds only on the wing and never on the ground. At daybreak, a large group of doves flew above and over us toward the water tank. All three of us took shots.

With a double-barreled shotgun, you have a second chance. But once the doves heard the gunshots, they flew in a swift zigzag fashion that made another hit impossible. Doves flew over almost every minute. Cato and his friend did well, hit at least a dozen or more each. I shot two boxes of shells and hit none.

Cato dropped me at the drugstore to open it up. We were over fifteen minutes late. A few customers were by the door. Instead of being irate about waiting, they asked, "How was the dove hunt?" Because of this and other incidents, it was clear to me how important the sports of hunting and fishing were in local people's lives. In fact, stories of hunting and fishing dominated my casual talks with the local men.

It was also clear to me that I wasn't capable of being a hunter, as much as I tried. Nevertheless, hunting and fishing provided the topics that dominated my conversation with others in this town. They also gave me the excuse to be outdoors in nature, something that I have always loved. Of the two sports, being out around a lake or a stream with a rod and reel was the more intriguing.

I befriended Jim, a cowboy-type young man who may have never been on a horse in his life. He came to the store, wearing a beat-up dusty cowboy hat and scuffed cowboy boots, an oversized, tarnished silver belt buckle conspicuous on his lanky frame. He was an avid fisherman and our talk always focused on fishing. He sold me an aluminum boat with a motor and a trailer at a price I couldn't refuse and instructed me to buy fishing tackle suitable for trolling and other tackle for offshore fishing. I had a hitch installed on my reliable pickup to pull the boat and trailer.

Karen and I decided to fish in a lake not too far from Gallup. Still a novice at driving, I worried about backing up at landing docks on a busy morning while seasoned boatmen patiently waited. Karen gave me directions to turn the steering wheel left or right. Flustered, in the attempt to back into the water to unload, I would almost always jackknife the boat trailer.

Once in the water, we trolled and caught fish, almost our limit. The fish warden showed up and wanted to check our catch to be sure we hadn't gone over our trout limit. Karen proudly pulled out the string of fish we dangled on the side of the boat to keep our catch cool and fresh. He looked at the fish and with a smile advised us to throw those fish back in the water and to follow him. It turned out the fish we caught earlier were what they called "trash fish"—bony fish that weren't suitable for the table. Not one of them was a trout. He said he would show us where to fish for bluegills. The warden, proud to give advice to two wannabe fisher-people, assured us there was no limit on bluegills. "They are great eating," he vouched. He said that we'd have a great time. He departed, wishing us the best.

The bluegills ran in colonies. New fisher-people as we

were, we still caught quite a few. We strung them on a chain that we laid against the side of our aluminum boat. While hooking her bluegill on the chain, the chain slipped out of Karen's hand and disappeared into the deep-blue-green, soupy water. She looked at me.

"No way," I said. "They're gone!"

———

During our stay in Gallup, I set my artistic aspirations to a minimum, but I still managed to dabble in painting, trying to learn the craft. There were no art supply stores in town other than small craft stores, where I found some basic oil paints and a children's watercolor pan box. I managed to do small figurative paintings in oil done from memory, one of which Cato and his wife showed interest in, so I offered it to them as a gift.

Over the four years I worked for Cato Drugs, it became clear to me that Gallup was no place for a hopeful artistic destination. Yet in this town, the most memorable and profound turning point in my life happened. I applied for US citizenship, studied the Constitution, and passed the exam. I became a citizen of the United States of America and have never been more proud.

At some point, it became necessary for us to find a place where we'd spend the rest of our lives, inspired by and content in our surroundings—a place we could call our permanent dreamland-homeland. Gallup, or even the state of New Mexico, wasn't such a place. I also wanted to be where I believed it was still possible to become an artist.

In the summer of 1965, we took an investigatory trip

to look for a promising state or a town to call our own. We planned to sleep in our pickup camper. Since neither one of us was a seasoned camper, every few days we intended to take a room in a hotel to clean up and rest while driving around the country.

From looking at magazines, two states were attractive and promising: Colorado and Oregon. Denver, Colorado, was an artistic city, the first on our itinerary. We camped close to a lake, where mosquitos the size of wasps stung us through our thick Levi's and kept us awake all night. The next morning, we found Denver flooded. Water covered the roads.

After over an hour of detours in uncharted directions, our maddening experience led us out of the city and to our next promising state, Oregon. To our delight, our scouting trip was an eye-opener. The information about the state that we had discovered in magazines proved real. In different areas of the state, the landscapes and towns varied in appearance and climatic conditions, yet we loved every town we visited or passed through.

We arrived in Eugene and decided that somewhere around there would be our permanent homeland. And we never looked back. Eugene had a university, an artistic presence, a moderate climate, green countryside, and a place where I could grow flower and vegetable gardens similar to my childhood imaginary landscapes.

Back in Gallup, we saved and planned our move but had not divulged our intent to anyone, not even Ira Cato. I planned to give him a month's notice, more than adequate time for him to find a replacement. Since he had relied on me for four years, I needed time to figure out how to let him know we had decided to move away.

When I disclosed our intent, it caught him by a total surprise. His explosive anger baffled me. Seething, with a furious look on his face, he gestured at the door, "You want to leave? Hand me the keys and leave now."

And so I was fired.

PART III

OREGON

CHAPTER 9

The Promised Land

As long as I have been a pharmacist, I have tried to do my best for my employers. Yet I was an unhappy man working in towns that had no artistic presence, biding my time in utmost discontent. I wondered how many years it would take until my dreams and hopes and ultimate happiness would be possible. I reminded myself that success in the arts, even with hard work and self-motivation, didn't mean financial independence.

Some artists rely on someone else's financial assistance, or they have the talent to market their own art, and most teach. Neither Karen nor I imagined relying on someone else's financial help, and neither of us is endowed with marketing talent. In my obsession to become an artist, my pharmacy career at some point had to end. Churning in my mind was a vision that there might be another way for financial independence that would still allow me to pursue the life of the artist. A way that would facilitate rather than obstruct my artistic dream without placing a burden on my family. And in the glorious state of Oregon, I envisioned my utopia where I could live my fantasy.

We were abandoning our permanent jobs, and moving to a new state, where we knew no one. We would be in a difficult situation, both unemployed, with only a few hundred dollars in savings. Yet our commitment to move was steadfast.

The New Mexico Board of Pharmacy and the Oregon Board allowed pharmacists' reciprocation between the two states, with a requirement to comply with the laws of the state the pharmacist was relocating to. In my case, that meant I needed to pass the Oregon Board of Pharmacy exam. To take the test, I had to be in Oregon in person.

Karen had a few months left of her New Mexico teaching contract. Since I was now unemployed, we decided I would drive to Oregon on my own to obtain my pharmacy license and find employment.

Our pickup still carried the wooden camper I had built and would be problematic in windy or snowy areas. Instead, I hitched our aluminum boat trailer to Karen's car and loaded it with as much as I could—small, necessary items like kitchen stuff, the army cot I used in Los Alamos, and lawn chairs—and fastened a heavy-duty tarp over the boat. Although I had been driving for several years now, I still dreaded driving even in the best of conditions, let alone a long-distance trip in February through unfamiliar highways and possible snowy stretches.

It wasn't long before I faced deep snow. More kept falling, and visibility was only a few feet. Sometimes I wasn't sure I was even on the road. I kept my eyes on a visible string of telephone poles, a clue that I wasn't driving in a pasture. The boat often fishtailed, and I wondered if it might swerve off the road and drag the car and me into a ditch where I'd freeze to death in what seemed like a forsaken land. The wipers strained to shovel the piled-up snow off the windshield. I kept reproaching myself for my stupidity. Why didn't I wait until spring? Karen and I could have had a pleasant, hopeful drive.

The sign welcoming me to Oregon elicited a thrilling sensation, as if I were in heaven. I drove on I-5 North flanked by green fields against distant blue-purple hills, pastures peppered by white sheep, grazing cattle, and horses, reminding me of the vivid green mounds of moss by the irrigation barrel of my childhood. Now, my childhood fantasies seemed to materialize in real life.

Joe Powell, Karen's principal, and his wife, Maryanne, had also planned to move to Oregon. Maryanne had driven with her adolescent daughters to find a house in Roseburg while Joe fulfilled his contract obligation in Gallup. He had already been hired as a principal in Riddle, a small town near Roseburg. We had planned that I would visit Maryanne on my way to Eugene. Maryanne's friend in Roseburg had a vacant lot where Maryanne said I could park my boat, stay the night in Roseburg, then drive to Eugene the following morning. Once settled, I could drive down and pick up my boat. I took her up on the offer and appreciated her generosity and friendship, relieved that I wouldn't have to drive on unfamiliar roads in Eugene or find parking spots while pulling the boat.

In Eugene, staying in a motel for long would have been costly. The money we had saved had to last. In the *Register-Guard*, the only major newspaper in Eugene, I found a room listed for rent at just forty dollars per month. *Such a low monthly payment for a room and access to a kitchen is amazingly perfect*, I thought.

I found the house with the room on Tenth Avenue among a group of similar old homes that had moss-covered roofs. The thick moss on the roofs reminded me of Van Gogh's paintings of thatched-roof cottages. It was a two-story, dilapidated house with faded olive-green siding and rust-colored trim that in another life may have been white. There was a small, mowed lawn. I walked toward the front door, past a few yellow and purple crocuses huddled under two overgrown rose bushes with mildew-covered leaves, and I knocked.

While I waited patiently for the door to open, I couldn't help but wonder how the house had aged. What was left of the crusty paint on the doorjamb hung on for dear life, and the cedar shingles appeared to twist in agony. A shriveled-looking old man, over eighty years old with gray, thin hair and a beard (and one front tooth missing!), greeted me with a gentle smile.

He said he was the landlord and would show me the room. We climbed rickety narrow stairs, which squeaked and groaned, up to a room with a high bed and an upholstered chair with a stained maroon velvet covering. There was hardly space to walk around. *It's perfect,* I thought.

The kitchen was in a corner of the house. An old man, holding a coffee cup with both hands, stood in a space that might accommodate one or two standing people. There was an old-fashioned stove caked with grease. On it was a stained coffee pot. "This is Bob," my landlord said.

With shaky hands, Bob put down the cup on the narrow counter and shook my hand.

"Welcome," he said.

I paid the landlord, went to my room, and sat on the chair. *What's next?*

Before long, each of the men living in the house had come to visit and welcome me. They were all over eighty, with one even in his nineties! Bob brought me a portable radio and insisted that it would keep me company since he could see I had little to entertain me. I thanked him, but there was no need for a radio. "I read a lot," I said.

He looked around the room and said that the lighting was bad and reading would ruin my eyes. He handed me the radio anyway.

I was thirty-three years old then, and they appreciated my presence among them. They considered me their friend, and I was a good listener to their stories. Sometimes in the evenings, they brought coffee and cookies they wanted to share while we talked.

I had scheduled an appointment with the Oregon Board of Pharmacy to take my State of Oregon Pharmacy Law exam. I passed the written exam and gained registered pharmacist status in Oregon.

Since I had acquired my employment in both Farmington and Gallup through McKesson's recommendations, I again reached out to them for assistance in finding work in Eugene. They said that a local drugstore in a small shopping center on Highway 99 needed a pharmacist, and I jotted down the address.

Until that time, I had never looked for a job in person or had an interview with an employer. Just the thought of being interviewed face-to-face made me cringe. I have always wondered why it was so painful for me to talk to people, whether in a group or one at a time. When it came to seeking employment as a pharmacist, I surmised my anxiety must have been due to my lack of skill in conversing with others. Although I did well as a pharmacist and my employers appreciated and had full trust in my work, I always felt like a fake since my heart wasn't in the job.

I drove on Highway 99 to the Gilbert Shopping Center, which had four or five small shops besides the small drugstore I was looking for. The store had a pharmacy and a small sundries area. When I entered, a young pharmacist was behind the counter. I asked him if he was the owner.

He said, no, that he was hired only a week before and that the owner would be at the pharmacy the next day.

Although I was disappointed that I didn't get the job, I was relieved I hadn't gone through the discomfort of asking the owner about hiring me, only to be told he had already hired a pharmacist.

I continued my drive on Highway 99 north toward Junction City. It was a cool morning. The sun peeked on and off through thin, silvery clouds that streaked above my windshield. Green pastures stretched for miles on both sides of the highway. A few scrub oaks stood here and there in pastures along water drainage gullies. Horses and cattle were grazing in pastures, and white sheep dotted the landscape. In the far distance on the right side of the highway was a violet hill that had the silhouette of a saddle. Many years later, I discovered that a columnist had initiated a contest in the Willamette Valley to name the hill. The Saddle won.

Right before entering Junction City, I took Highway 36 west and drove eight miles on a straight two-lane highway to the small town of Cheshire. I stopped at a small convenience store for a box of chocolate cookies and a Pepsi. Other than the small store, Cheshire had a post office and a gas station. I checked my map for sites I could investigate. The Long Tom River and Fern Ridge Lake were in proximity. Since I had all the time to drive around, enthralled by the surrounding beauty, I took Territorial Highway, then turned on Meadowview Road and drove until I reached the point where the Long Tom River crossed the highway. I parked by the bridge. Fantastic scenery of pastures and hills was all around. The river cut under the highway and meandered through the landscape on both sides. On the right bank, it formed a small pool with still water reflecting the sky and adjacent hills while refracting the fallen branches and twigs on its bank.

Memories of my early childhood came to mind—of our home on Jabal Amman (Amman Hill) when I was around seven years old. In Amman, vegetation was scarce, as was water. The only flowers I saw were in home gardens, including ours.

When I wasn't at school, there wasn't much to occupy my aloneness. At one end of our house, under the grape arbor, I spent most of my time in a dreamy state of mind, concocting imaginary scenes. Next to the water barrel on one end of the house, over a small area of clumps of soil that were moist from careless water spills, mounds of lime green moss grew. In my imagination, they formed green hills and meadows where sheep grazed and horses galloped. To complete these fanciful scenes, I carved a stream bed in the soil with a sturdy twig and poured a cupful of water into the indentation. In my mind, it was a pond that had a variety of colorful fish.

Around Eugene, there was no shortage of water. The Willamette River flowed through the city, but more enticing was this gentle river in the quietness of the countryside and its lazy roll over silt. There was no rushing sound of angry water, only the soothing sound of water gliding gently and swirling around rocks here and there.

I crossed over to the other side of the bridge and walked on a dirt path along the river. There were luscious wildflowers all over the bank. A man sat on a stool down by the stream, casting his line upstream and watching it float downstream. He looked up and waved.

Consulting my map, I drove to Kirk Park. It was across the highway from the manmade Fern Ridge Lake. Water spilled over a dam, forming a stream and a pond by the park. At the park, I walked on trails along the bank of the pond, then sat on a picnic bench, enjoying the views all around me. There was no one around and the serenity was mesmerizing. Occasionally, fish jumped with a splash, breaking the tranquility and rippling the otherwise mirror-like face of the pond that reflected the blue sky. I was startled to hear a voice. A man with a dog came by and wanted to talk. After learning that I had just moved from New Mexico and that I was a painter—it was the first time I'd ever mentioned this out loud to anyone but Karen—he said, "At Fern Ridge Lake, on the other side of the highway, there are two parks for sailing and picnicking." But he preferred the park we were in since hardly anyone came there. Some preferred the other parks, and because I was a painter, he thought I might find those parks more picturesque with great subjects to paint.

Not too far down the highway was the popular park the man mentioned. A few sailboats were anchored by the bank.

Tarps of white and blue covered the boats. And here again, there was no one around. I took out a small pocket notebook and drew a group of boats against a backdrop of firs on the far bank of the lake.

I treasured my leisurely drives around Eugene, invigorated by the beauty of the landscape around me and swept up by the conviction that this is where I would build on my artistic ambition. It was imperative that I focus on learning the craft of painting. Purchasing art supplies became my priority.

At the Oregon Art Supply Store on Pearl Street in Eugene, I was intoxicated by the art materials on the shelves just like the "kid in a toy shop" cliché—although I don't remember ever getting a toy in my childhood that transported me to experience that sensation. Dazzling paints—oils, watercolors, acrylics, and pastels—were displayed. I bought a black folding metal Holbein watercolor palette, a few tubes of primary colors, and a couple of earth colors. I bought a size-twelve sable watercolor brush and, for detail work, a rigger brush. A couple of sheets of watercolor paper and a board to clip the paper on completed my purchase. I paid a fortune, yet I was in a state of euphoria. With these beautiful virgin supplies on hand, I was motivated to paint my impression of the seductive landscape all around me.

Back in my room, I placed all my art materials on the bed and looked at them for a long time. I ripped each watercolor paper into eight pieces. The small size would make it easier to paint a quick sketch, and I would have more practice papers. From there on, I would focus on practicing rather than finishing pieces.

Charged with emotion, I stayed awake until late at night and woke up early in the morning to look at my treasure. Holding each painting tool that lay on the chair by my bed took me outdoors in my mind—painting the pools formed around the Long Tom River, the twigs, fallen branches, and the shimmering reflections in the water.

The next day at 10 a.m., I visited the McKesson branch in Eugene. Did they know of other pharmacy openings? "Yes, Tiffany's Drugstore on Franklin Boulevard," the man at the desk said, and wrote down the address. I remembered seeing the store the day I arrived in Eugene.

The pharmacist in his white jacket stood behind the pharmacy counter, talking to his assistant, a young woman engrossed in his story. As I approached them, he stopped his chat.

"I'm a pharmacist from New Mexico," I said.

"Welcome. I got a call from McKesson and was expecting you. I'm Fred and this is Vonnie, our valued partner."

He opened the swinging door, stepped down and wrapped his arm around my shoulder. We walked to the office to meet Mr. Kurtz, the store manager. With a few pleasant words, Mr. Kurtz welcomed me as Fred's right-hand pharmacist. I was so relieved to have the major burden of seeking employment lifted from my shoulders after only a few days in Eugene.

With his cheerful attitude and sincere smile, Fred was attentive to man, woman, young, or old. From the day I stepped behind the pharmacy counter of Tiffany's Drugstore, we developed a close working relationship that lasted many years. He appreciated my work ethic as a pharmacy partner as well as our friendship—finding it easy to talk to me about his love for hunting, fishing, and winter skiing—and of our mutual love for the state of Oregon.

Fred was a dedicated pharmacist, but unlike me, socializing was his talent. He preferred it over the prescription-filling routine. Like Ada, Vonnie was indispensable. She answered phone calls cheerfully and created a comfortable working atmosphere.

Having confidence that my employment was permanent, I wanted to get involved in the Oregon art scene. Oregon has a large art community. Eugene has the University of Oregon, an art museum, two art associations, and three art supply stores. Portland has art colleges, the Portland Art Museum, and several art supply stores. It also has the Watercolor Society of Oregon.

I became a member of the two art associations in the Eugene area: the Emerald Art Center in Springfield, a small town across the Willamette River from Eugene, and Maude Kerns Art Center, which was within walking distance from my workplace. I intended to take part in open studio sessions and meet a few local artists and when possible, enroll in a painting class. I signed up to do volunteer gallery-sitting at the Emerald Art Center whenever I had a day off. The center had a small gallery of members' paintings and an extensive art library. On days that I gallery-sat, I brought my watercolor palette, brushes, and paper with me. Because I was a beginner, any original art such as the members' watercolors exhibited on the walls was inspiring for me. But what was more beneficial were the library books I could check out—monograms of past artists and how-to books on painting in a variety of media.

At the art center, being on my own in total stillness, surrounded by art and art books, I did a few watercolor sketches. Sometimes, someone showed up to view the members' artwork. It gave me the chance to talk about art with art enthusiasts. When they glanced at my sketches, I explained I was a beginner yet a passionate art lover. Without commenting, they would move on.

The watercolor medium was quite popular with many Oregon artists. A group of California watercolor artists, such as Robert E. Wood, Morris Shubin, Milford Zornes, and Dong Kingman, had promoted and elevated the medium to a high standard. Each, in his own style, achieved a personal impression of the landscape and not a rendered copy as the realists did. This appealed to me but wasn't easy to accomplish. A few of these artists published how-to watercolor books that, for a while, became my primary source of inspiration and information. At the time, there were no videos to enable me to watch an artist do a painting and learn about his or her painting process. Printed dull images and texts in how-to books provided me a little guidance. Soon, I concluded that I must have the self-motivation to paint as often as I could and not focus on any particular method of painting. Then, in an intuitive approach through successes and failures, I might find a personal style of my own.

To become a member of the prestigious Watercolor Society of Oregon was the aspiration and goal of all local watercolor artists. Membership admittance required a high standard of proficiency. The watercolor society had twice-yearly competitions, juried by California master artists. The exhibits of the selected work would travel through the large cities in Oregon. Since I had a full-time job, it wasn't easy for me to view any of them in faraway cities. When one of the exhibits reached Eugene, I viewed it several times, spellbound, inspired, and energized by what I saw on the walls of the gallery. I went home and told myself that someday my painting would be among the works in such an exhibition.

When I became a member of the Maude Kerns Art Center, I enrolled in the two open studio sessions. When I had the afternoon-evening pharmacy shift, I participated in the morning Painting from Life session. At the end of the session, I would drive to nearby Hendricks Park, eat my sandwich, and get to work at 1 p.m. When I had the full-day pharmacy shift, I joined the evening open studio drawing sessions at Lawrence Hall at the University of Oregon.

Finding myself among established artists gave me a feeling of belonging I hadn't felt in the past. I was in a state of euphoria, a different person altogether. Although painting required decisive paint application with every brushstroke, I was never under stress. It had already become a way of life vital to my well-being. I was confident that becoming an artist was my destiny, otherwise I would be an unhappy man. I promised myself that a day would come when I would be a full-time artist. I possessed the self-motivation, energy, and passion to get there. But then there was always that nagging question: *When will it happen, and how long will I have to wait?*

CHAPTER 10

Home on Josephine Street

Having permanent employment was quite a relief. For over three weeks, I had been living with my old-timer friends on Tenth Street. Once I secured a job, I looked for rental listings in the *Register-Guard*. My initial aim was to rent an apartment or even a house. Then, on a whim, I looked at houses for sale. A house on Josephine Street in the River Road area of Eugene attracted my attention.

When the Realtor took me to the site, I found a most appealing home in a quiet neighborhood, close to schools, parks, and shopping venues. A welcoming, attractive front porch with a trellis covered with a gorgeous evergreen clematis greeted me. And when she unlocked the door, I was confident that the criteria Karen and I would have wanted to see in a house—warm and inviting—was unquestionably present. It was a three-bedroom home with a kitchen, bathroom, family room, front garden with a white picket fence, and a large, fenced backyard. In 1966, its purchase price of $16,000 was reasonable and mortgage payments were within our budget. What kept our marriage harmonious was that we respected each other's likes and dislikes. In the past, in important situations that affected both of us, but we didn't have the opportunity to consult each other, Karen and I trusted the other to make the right decision. I seized the opportunity, and Karen and I became homeowners for the first time in our lives.

Even with empty rooms, the house was comfortable in every respect. The family room was a favorite of mine, where I spent my evenings sitting on a picnic chair, reading or listening to music on the small radio I purchased to keep me company. But more importantly, I spent my evening hours painting in this room. In the corner of the living room, I placed the army cot that was my bed, adequate for at least a couple of months until I could take the bus to New Mexico, arrange for a mover to transport our furniture, then drive with Karen to Oregon and our new home.

I took photos of our new home, inside and out, to send to Karen.

Our new next-door neighbors, Bill Kunkle and his wife, Marvel, came by to welcome me. From our first conversation, we developed a long-lasting friendship. It turned out that Bill and I had a mutual love for the arts. He was passionate about photography.

I disappointed my old housemates on Tenth Street when I told them I was moving out. Every one of the five elderly men came to bid me goodbye and good luck. Ever since, I've held pleasant memories of that old house and its old men, and often that small room comes to mind. For years, when I drove down Tenth Street, I looked up to see the room on the second floor, wondering who was sleeping there and how many of my old friends were still alive. This room had appeared at a crucial time in my life, relieving me, at least temporarily, of some of my worries.

When Karen and I completed our move, we were ecstatic to be in Eugene together. The movers unloaded the many boxes and the furniture they hauled from Gallup. Not willing to tackle the unopened boxes, I drove Karen through the countryside around Eugene to impress her with the beauty of the landscape.

It was an afternoon in June, and we were driving on roads I had already discovered when it began to rain and wouldn't let up. The wipers agonized over coping with the buckets of water being dumped on us. I couldn't see through the windshield. Gullies in fields that were barely full a few days earlier burst their banks, and water spilled over the fields and onto the highway, creating lakes I had to drive through.

This gripped me with worries. What if Karen, facing the miserable conditions we were experiencing, regretted our decision to take such a drastic gamble? We'd believed that the weather in Oregon was temperate, with sporadic drizzles possible, but that wouldn't prevent us from being outdoors. We hadn't expected to need the heavy coats we'd brought with us from Gallup. Could it be this torrential rain was the norm that, in haste, we had missed in our research of Oregon's Willamette Valley? A clerk's remark at Cato's pharmacy came to mind: "Oregon? Is that where you're moving? I understand moss will grow on your back in no time!"

It wasn't long before the rain stopped, the water receded from the roads and fields back into the gullies, and the sun came out. The lush beauty of Oregon emerged. Gone were my brief fears, and we were never in doubt of our commitment again.

Early in 1967, another company bought Tiffany's Drugstore. The sequence was a bit murky. Fred went to work for Valu-Mart drugstore on River Road and asked me to go along with him. I did.

After only a few months of working for Valu-Mart, Karen and I made plans to take a vacation and visit my parents in Amman. We had around $5,000 in savings, and I thought it was the right time to go. My parents were getting old, and it was time to fulfill the promise to return home I had made to my mother on the day of my departure to the US. I regretted that while I was at UNM, I did not write them to tell them I was doing fine. When by chance I got news from home through a visiting friend who had come from Jordan, my mother asked if I would write and tell her how I was doing, even if it was a few words on a postcard. I was so absorbed in my problems at the time that I ignored her pleas. During the subsequent years when she knew I was married and settled in the US, her pleas ceased altogether. She must have surmised that I was doing well and was happy with my life in the country that I had come to adopt as my own.

Our trip would also be a good experience for Karen to visit that part of the world, meet my family, and witness first-hand what I had told her about my childhood home and the country where I was born. I imagined my mother's excitement when I heard she had the inside walls of our house white-washed to make it hospitable for our arrival.

The US government required that travelers to the Middle East have a few mandatory vaccinations for a variety of foreign diseases. Karen and I complied. We had our passports and visas in order and were just a week from our departure in early June 1967 when the war between the Arab countries and Israel erupted. The US government advisory stressed that traveling to any of the Middle Eastern countries was unsafe. The plans for our trip vanished.

Soon after, the clerks at Valu-Mart joined the union and went on strike. Although as pharmacists Fred and I weren't unionized and had no reason to participate in the strike, Fred decided we should go on strike in solidarity with the clerks to put pressure on the management. Pharmacy law stated that a drugstore with a pharmacy open to the public cannot do business without a pharmacist on duty. I was ambivalent about the situation. On the one hand, I couldn't afford to lose my job, but felt I couldn't go against Fred's decision.

While Fred stayed away from the picket line; I chose to picket along with the clerks for the duration. All my life, I had hated being in the limelight, and here I presented myself as a troublemaker when the whole affair didn't even concern me. It was a new and excruciating experience.

When the strike ended in favor of the employees, the managers were furious, and Fred and I endured the brunt of their wrath. Since management controlled whether we had a clerk to help at the pharmacy, when we called for one to tend to the cash register during our busy hours, the appeal fell on deaf ears. We did our best to keep things as amiable as possible. Nevertheless, the canceled trip Karen and I had been looking forward to, the harrowing picketing experience I had no reason to be part of, and the hectic state that ensued at work heightened my need to find another way to gain financial independence to pursue my goal.

Throughout my pharmacy career, I had continued to

practice the craft of painting whenever I could, and it had become a costly activity. I was extravagant with my painting materials. I believed that the only way to learn the craft was to paint a lot with the best material I could afford.

I had heard of "living off the land," a way of life advocated by free-spirited communities. Although it seemed to me a far-fetched idea, in my exasperation, I pondered its viability. What if I bought a piece of land and built a house, doing all the construction myself? The cost would be a fraction of a house built by a contractor. What if I farmed the land, and the produce provided self-sufficiency and brought in some income? Was that a preposterous idea? I hadn't even questioned my qualifications yet. I hadn't considered what building a house entailed. I mentioned my intention to a neighbor. "Do you know how many boxes of nails go into framing a house?" he asked.

The more I thought about this, the more obsessed I became. I concluded it was my only option.

Karen had only a vague idea of my intentions, but she went along without reservation. On weekends, we drove around, keeping our eyes open for rural properties for sale.

On one of our excursions, we drove west on Highway 36, past Cheshire, the small town I passed through during my first few days in Eugene. We exited onto Hall Road. Half a mile onward and on the left side of the road, we saw a sign: "Six Acres for Sale." I parked our pickup in a gravel parking space. There were no visible fenced boundaries we could see. Wild roses and brambles covered a wire fence along Hall Road.

Rye grass pasture lay for a distance. At the horizon, a hillside rose to the skyline. We took a walk toward the hill. At its base, there was a gulley filled with slow-moving, shallow water. Along its bank were a couple of wild apple trees in bloom, a few bushes and brambles, and lilac and white wildflowers. Finches flittered on the branches of the apple trees.

My eyes focused on the gentle waves of the tentacles of vegetation reflected in the silvery flow of water. A red dragonfly zipped over the surface. And I wondered if there were minnows I couldn't see, dashing happily beneath the surface. The thought of those tireless little gems brought to mind a stream from my childhood in Russeifa, a village a few kilometers from Amman, where my family and I often picnicked. It wasn't the village itself on the hill with its few adobe homes, or the Arab children kicking a can, playing soccer in its dusty alleys that kept me awake the nights before our planned picnics—it was the haunting little stream, in the lowland, just like what we saw here in this gulley, only deeper.

Memories of those picnics have stayed with me ever since. I still remember how, at a spot shaded by bamboo, shrubs, and some fruit trees, not unlike these trees that flanked this gulley, my mother spread blankets and brought out food baskets. My father placed a couple of watermelons in the stream to keep them cool. Mesmerized by the sights and sounds, I would crouch by the bank as the gentle water glided over colorful pebbles and sand. Close to my feet, the shallow water seemed to stand still. Sometimes I'd see a single dry bamboo leaf floating like a lost canoe on the glassy surface. It would hesitate for a moment, then continue its peaceful journey. There were tiny crabs in the stream that shot out from their hideaways, skipping sideways along the bottom, dislodging sand particles.

Long-winged dragonflies zigzagged above the surface of the water, as if performing a ritual exercise. It was all a thrilling sight, a haven for tiny creatures in and out of the water. A reflection of a cluster of bamboo canes and thick brush across the stream shimmered. Tiny birds preened on tops of canes that gently swayed in the breeze in perpetual waves. But what gave me a rush were the minnows that swarmed by my toes, darting in unison as if on a mission, their silvery sides reflecting rays of the sun that found their way through the canes to form patterns on the surface of the water.

During one picnic, I pled with my sister Alexandra to assist me in collecting a few minnows to take home and put in our irrigation barrel. We stood knee-high in the water across from each other, each holding two knotted corners of a white handkerchief that we spread a few inches below the surface. And with eyes focused, unheeded by the strain on our backs, we waited with patience while my heart pounded in anticipation. It wouldn't be long before a few minnows, unimpressed by our trap, would pass over our handkerchief. With a quick response, lifting the kerchief in a swift swoop, we trapped a couple of fish in our shallow pool of water.

My father helped us transfer the fish and some water into a jar that I wedged between rocks at the shallow end of the stream. All that afternoon, I kept my eyes on the fish that finally settled down, their fins fanning at leisure. On our way home, as much as I tried to steady the jar I held on my lap, water spilled all over my shorts with every bump on the road. At home, I eased the minnows into one of the irrigation barrels at one end of our home. Every morning after, I would look for them, hoping that in their new home they would be content—as if they weren't only in a stream but in a large lake—to grow big and multiply. To my delight, they seemed to move in tandem inches below the surface. But then one day, to my dismay, I found them floating motionless on their sides.

Karen had heard these stories in the past, but now she realized my ardent affection toward nature and its waters was not only to its streams, lakes, and ponds but even to this simple, unpretentious country spillway.

Picking a lilac, she turned to me. "Let's walk up the hill to see what's up there."

Over logs that crossed the gulley, we walked to the other side and climbed the steep hill to where it leveled off. Around 300 feet from where we stood on the hill, there was another sign: "Six Acres for Sale." It also had a map outlining the land—a perfect rectangle. At the top of the hill was an access road that led to Highway 36.

Looking back in the direction we had come from was a spectacular view. From where we stood, the land dipped to the gulley where Karen had picked the lilac she still held in her hand. Past the ryegrass field, past where we parked our pickup, and past Hall Road were vast fields stretching for miles toward blue-green hills of fir trees.

"What a spectacular view," I said. "I'd love to build a house right here where we're standing."

On the west side, beyond the property's boundary line, the land sloped to where a house was being built. A man looked up and waved, then walked up to say hello.

"Hi, I'm Forrest, but they call me Jack. My wife is Bunny," he said. "Are you thinking of buying this land? If you do, welcome to the neighborhood."

He pointed to an old white farmhouse with a couple of white barns on the west side of the road close to the highway and said it was the Thompsons' property. And on the east side, there was a white spec house that the landowner, Mr. Allen, had built when he parceled his land. Next to his property, Jack said, was the Hibbards' house.

We thanked him for the information and walked down to our pickup. I phoned the Realtor the next morning and planned to meet her at the top of the hill.

This time we took Highway 36 and drove to the top of the property, where we found her waiting for us. She showed us the metal markers on the two corners of the property and said there were other metal posts at the lower corners by Hall Road.

"Six acres for $6,000 is a great buy, and the owner is selling it for a low down payment and monthly payments of just $50. Think about it and let me know."

"We'll buy it," I told the Realtor the following morning. We signed the papers, and we were landowners. As soon as we signed the contract, I knew I was at a thrilling juncture in my life.

CHAPTER 11

Ownership

Karen never questioned the absurdity of acquiring a bare piece of land and building a house on it with hardly any savings to finance it, or the responsibility of building it myself despite having no knowledge of what building construction entailed.

Once we bought the land, I devised a plan. The first task was to build fences to give us a sense of ownership and to set the property apart from the adjacent pastures and contain any livestock we might acquire. At this time, the parcel was lost amid fields of ryegrass with no boundary markers.

I rented a heavy metal post driver to drive posts between railroad anchors. On weekends, Karen drove the pickup while I stood on its bed and hammered in posts at eight-foot intervals all along the perimeter of the land. We attached sheep fencing over the metal posts and a strand of barbwire above it. It took us a few weekends to install the fences around the land as well as cross fencing with a gate to keep livestock off the area where I intended to build our house.

Once we had our property fenced, we needed a well and electricity to run a pump. For outdoor electrical service, I dug in a post and hung a meter box complying with the power company's specifications, so we had electricity hooked up.

Our neighbor, Jack, recommended a man named Jasper to drill our well. He drilled on the west side of the land, at a distance from Jack's fence line. He reached a level of 130 feet. "It's a good well," he said.

He installed the casing, pipe, and submersible pump. I dug a trench from the electrical post to the well site and lay in electrical ground wire. Once the pump was in operation, my worries dispelled that we wouldn't find water or have enough of it to water all the future fruit trees, berries, and flowers I wanted to have on our land.

Then I needed to build a pumphouse. It would be the first building project I had undertaken in my life. I had no idea how builders constructed a wood-framed house, nor what was between the painted siding and the inner wall.

At the Eugene library, I found a how-to home construction book applicable to houses in the Northwest. It included how to frame walls and gables, as well as how to build a concrete foundation.

I bought an electric, handheld Black+Decker circular saw, four steel sawhorses, and eight-foot lengths of two-by-fours.

I planned to pour a concrete slab foundation to enclose the well casing. Rather than mix the aggregates myself on site with a shovel or rent a concrete mixer, in my naivete, I thought it'd be much easier to haul the ready-mixed concrete from a concrete company in Eugene. That was a big mistake.

By the time I drove to our place, the gravel component of the mix had settled. It took over an hour of arduous effort to remix the semi-hardened concrete with a shovel.

Shovelful by shovelful, I poured the concrete into the form that I had assembled around the perimeter of my project. I troweled and leveled the concrete around the well casing.

Then I covered it with plastic to provide a slow cure. Scraping and rinsing the hardened concrete that had filled the crevices in the joints of the cart was another major time-consuming problem.

Two days later, the slab was ready for framing. From the borrowed book, I learned the basic constructions of walls and rafters for a gable-roofed building. I followed the exact code requirement for framing homes. Although this was supposed to be an unassuming structure to protect the water tank and pipes from the elements, I gave it the respect of the modern-day, fancy home it deserved. For a decorative look, I bought black rocks from a nearby quarry on Ferguson Road in Junction City and built a rock wall skirting around the bottom part of the square building. It took research on how to do it to prevent the stones ever falling off the wall. I used nails spaced around the stones where I applied the grout. When the grout that covered the nails and the edges of the stones hardened, it kept the stones from pulling away from the plywood sheathing. The nails worked almost like rebar.

For the roof, I went overboard as well, applying cedar wood shingles used in luxurious homes in Central Oregon rather than the composition shingles used on homes I had seen around Eugene. My self-congratulatory status was deflated when I found that the use of cedar roofing instead of the composition roofing was a big mistake. In Western Oregon and in Lane County where we live, it's considered a fire hazard.

All said and done, my humble building project taught me how much effort it took to learn how to handle carpenter tools and the step-by-step rudiments of framing a wood structure—

not unlike learning to ride a bike before climbing on a Harley.

Our next projects were, first, making our place productive to provide us with fruit and vegetables throughout the year; and second, creating a glorious setting with a variety of subjects that would change over the years and throughout the seasons so I could practice the craft of painting without the need to travel in search of scenery.

We established an orchard of the common fruit trees and planted a patch of sixty blueberry bushes and a row of grape vines. We landscaped the land around where I planned to build our home. We planted oak trees, flowering trees and shrubs, and created a joyous flower garden.

We also allotted a large area for a vegetable garden. After I rototilled the garden site, it rained. To our surprise, on the surface of our rototilled soil, Indian arrowheads glistened, and in a few spots charcoal and ash pits appeared. Delighted that I may have been standing on land once inhabited by the Siuslaw or the Kalapuyans, I imagined a moonlit evening fire pit surrounded by men smoking their pipes and chanting. I almost heard their chants echo off the distant hills.

We amended our garden clay soil with loam and compost and added mint straw. There was a time when mint farms were everywhere in Lane County. Farmers around us planted mint, specifically for the mint oil they exported to foreign countries. When driving around the area, we passed acres of deep blue-green mint carpets that stretched out on both sides of the highway. In the cool morning or evening hours, the pungent scent permeated the air with an invigorating aroma.

In our garden, we planted all we could grow in the

Willamette Valley, even what I thought was exotic, such as Jerusalem artichokes, which I'd never heard of (I am not sure they have much to do with Jerusalem). Like potatoes, the tubers of the Jerusalem artichokes were formed underground. They grew in abundance and were delicious to snack on.

Karen became an avid gardener. I still remember seeing her on her knees, planting corn while the blackbirds followed, picking out some of the corn kernels that she had stuck an inch into the fertile ground. But, with birds in mind, she planted a few more than what's recommended. Later, she would can or freeze most of our vegetables and fruits. I built a fruit and vegetable dryer that used a lamp bulb. It worked fine, and she dried sliced apples and vegetables. When we were finished landscaping our land, establishing our orchard, and planting our garden, Karen and I had turned a slumbering piece of ryegrass land into an ever-changing productive and dazzling oasis.

Back in 1966, when I had driven from Gallup to Oregon and crossed the Oregon border, what attracted me most were the red barns with their unique gables and horses all over the countryside. During my childhood I had only seen horses twice in real life. And both times I was captivated by their elegance.

When I was seven or eight years old, I befriended Ghazi, a boy who lived within walking distance of our home on Jabal Amman. I often visited him, and we sat on the front steps of his home on the dusty road that passed our houses. I do not recall what we talked about, if we talked at all.

Once, while we were sitting on the steps, we sighted a

horseman riding a magnificent white horse. The Arabian horse had its head up, neck arched, alert and noble. Emir Talal, the father of the late King Hussein of Jordan, was taking his morning ride, a kind and humble man with a pleasant face, dressed in the native Arab garb. We stood at attention before he approached us and saluted the Emir, and he, with a broad smile, saluted us in return.

The second time I saw horses, I was twelve years old. One day, a Bedouin friend of my father who sold us butter saw me holding my pellet gun and aiming at a straight pin secured on the face of our rough stone wall. Intrigued, he asked if he could try it himself. This man had a formidable presence, with a rifle slung over his shoulder and a couple of bullet belts criss-crossed over his chest, yet he acted like a child wanting to play. My rifle seemed small in his huge hands. He found ample pleasure in his attempts at hitting the pin. A few months later, he invited us to visit his tent on the outskirts of Amman and spend a day with his family.

My sister Alexandra and I accompanied my father. Following the Bedouin's directions, we drove on a rocky, dusty road that weaved through rugged terrain. There were no trees, no vegetation, and no life except for lizards and snakes slith- ering in an arid habitat. We came upon a hill. High on the horizon, we glimpsed a horseman—an image that material- ized like an apparition. The bareback rider galloped down the hill, then waved for us to follow. On top of the hill was a tent that in the distance looked like a black ant. As we approached, cheerful children ran to greet us. A couple of horses, a camel, and a few goats grazed on sparse brush. Inside the spacious tent, we sat in a circle. The wife had cooked *mansaf* (a rice and meat dish). She served it under a dome set in the center of a flat tray. I watched the Bedouin eat by forming a ball of the rice and meat in the palm of one hand, then, in a swoop like a magician's sleight of hand, flinging the ball of mansaf into his mouth.

We spent time with their cheerful children among their camels, goats, and horses. They rode bareback, galloping around the tent, and wanted us to join. Their riding seemed effortless. I wanted so badly to try, but I am glad I didn't. I am not sure I could have stayed on a horse without falling. Nevertheless, not only the horses but also horseback riding have fascinated me ever since.

In Oregon, there are horses and horse ranches everywhere; horseback riding is a popular sport. So I thought: *Why not take lessons and live my childhood dream?* Karen and I started taking horseback riding lessons with Dave Hurtley at Dave and Judy's Riverview Horse Ranch in Junction City.

After taking a few lessons, I figured why not have a horse on our land so that we could ride any time we wished. But I would need a barn for it.

At that time, Fred had decided that we would work three days of twelve-hour shifts, take off four days, and alternate. That suited me well and provided me the time to do my building projects.

I planned a horse barn at the bottom part of our land, parallel to Jack's property and near the Hall Road fence line. It would give me experience tackling a much more extensive building project than the pumphouse.

Again, throughout the barn-building construction, I adhered to the exact building code. It would be a primer for my more ambitious and hopeful future house-building project. Instead of the concrete foundation used in house buildings, I chose to build the foundation using a two-tier cinder block wall, something more manageable for a novice's one-man building project.

On my days off from the pharmacy, I drove to the site and dug a trench two feet wide and a foot deep all around the perimeter of the planned foundation. A few times, a teenage kid riding his horse on Hall Road would come to see what I was up to. He would leave his horse loose standing by the road, the reins dropped to the ground. It stood content, munching on bits of grass on the shoulder of the road while cars and trucks zoomed by. *Wouldn't it be nice to have a horse like that?* I thought.

It took close to four weeks to dig the trench. I got a concrete company to pour the four-inch slab into the trench. The slab would support the cinder block foundation. It took me a day to get it leveled. I went home with ample certainty that once the slab hardened it would be ready for the cinder block walls.

Late afternoon the next day, I noticed the customers coming into the pharmacy had hair and jackets dripping wet. "It's pouring out there," one man said. And it rained all night long. I told myself not to worry—the concrete would have hardened by then and wouldn't wash away.

When I drove to the site in the morning, the rain had stopped, but I found the trench filled with at least six inches of water above the concrete slab. I had two choices: either bail the water out of the trench, which would have been a major time-consuming job, or wait for the water to dissipate through the sides of the trench and hope for no more rain. I chose the latter. It took more than a week for the concrete slab to clear and be dry enough to build the two-tier cinder block wall.

Since we didn't have electricity at the barn site, I had the lumber company deliver the wood to an area by the pump-house. I cut the studs at the pumphouse a few at a time and hauled them down to the barn site in my pickup. All night I would think about the building process, going through every step in my mind to be sure I did everything according to specifications.

I framed the walls flat on the ground. Then with Jack and another friend's help, we raised the walls on top of the cinder block foundation and fastened the cut gable rafters to the top of the walls. For the roof, I used composition shingles. I partitioned the building into two stalls and a tack room. Once I nailed the plywood siding, I saw the barn in its finished state—ready to be stained. It was an impressive structure that gave me enormous pride.

Early the next morning, I arrived at the site with cans of red stain. There was a sign stapled to the siding with a conspicuous handwritten note: "Stop construction. Call this number." It was signed by the building inspector.

All my hopes sank. What if the inspector did to me what he had done to Jack? All Jack had done was build an indoor partition for his house that wasn't essential to the structure of the house, but it didn't conform to the building code. The inspector made him tear out not only that particular wall but also an adjacent wall, just to make a point. What if the inspector made me tear down the barn? It would be a moral defeat and a financial disaster.

As soon as I got home, I dialed the inspector's number and had to wait on the line. Throughout those long and agonizing minutes, in my mind, I went over versions of what to say.

When he came on the line, I stated my understanding that the building code didn't apply to building barns in rural areas.

"It sure didn't look like a barn to me!" he said. I sat down for a few minutes, shaken but also relieved that my phone call satisfied the inspector, that the structure was indeed a barn and not a house, and I could proceed with my work.

Karen and I stained the exterior with a deep red Olympic stain and when we were done, even I thought that it would have been a cozy apartment if it had plumbing and electricity and house doors rather than barn doors. And I thought: *Why can't I build our house?*

A medical sales representative talked me into buying one of his daughter's horses, Starbuck. He said it was an easygoing gelding. I figured since we had our barn ready for a horse, why not?

To get water to the barn, I rented a handheld gas-powered trencher and dug a trench down the steep hill from the pumphouse all the way to the barn, around 700 feet. It was slow work. The trencher had a mind of its own. To get it to dig in a straight line was an impossibility. When I reached the barn and looked up, my trench snaked down the hill as it wished. It took three days to dig the trench, lay the tubing, and cover it with the dug-up soil.

Starbuck turned out to be a stubborn horse. He tried to throw me off his back whenever he could and succeeded twice. I want to say I got bucked off, but for him it was no more effort than shooing a pesky fly off his back, and I was flat on the ground. Every day, I would drive the twenty-five miles from our home in Eugene to the property to feed the horse and check the water supply. On my days off from work, I would saddle Starbuck and ride for a while. I knew if I didn't exercise him, I would be in an awful lot of trouble, and I wished to take riding him off my to-do list because riding him was hell.

One weekend, Karen and I went to our place to ride for a while. While I was on Starbuck, he stumbled in a gopher hole and fell on his side, trapping my leg under him. He lay there motionless. "Karen, do something," I shouted.

Horrified to witness the whole incident as if in slow motion, she looked petrified. She walked toward us while talking to him. Starbuck lifted his head and stood up as if it had just been a prank. I got myself off the ground, shaken but without a scratch. To give Starbuck the benefit of the doubt, my clumsiness as a novice rider may have added to him losing his balance.

Since buying the property, I wanted whatever we had on our land to be productive. At Dave's ranch, I saw a beautiful purebred sorrel quarter horse mare named Jeepers Creepers. With the horse trouble I had experienced, I still didn't have the sense to say enough is enough. What if I bought Jeepers and had her bred by Dave's champion registered stallion, Trouble's Joker? With that kind of breeding, I might sell the resultant filly or colt and make a profit. We bought Jeepers and had her bred by Joker. It was a long wait as we saw her belly get larger and larger.

In 1969, the Willamette Valley had the worst snow we've ever experienced. In a twenty-four-hour period, we had almost two feet of snow according to records, and we ended up with a total of four feet of snow in the valley. It was impossible to drive, so I walked to work. Valu-Mart was a distance from our home. It was harrowing to walk that distance in deep snow, but I had a responsibility to make it on time, and I did, only to find out it made little sense to the management to have the store open with no customers. They closed the store, and I had to trudge back home.

We worried about our horses, especially Jeepers. We phoned Jack, asking him to water the horses. The water at the barn had frozen. He called us later to say that Jeepers wouldn't drink, and she seemed stressed. Karen called Dr. Moye, our very kind veterinarian, and explained the situation. He offered to look at Jeepers, and Karen rode with him in his vehicle equipped for driving in heavy snow. He had a way to warm up the water that took care of the horse's needs, and the purebred survived the ordeal.

Driving back and forth to our land to water the trees and our expansive vegetable garden and tend to our horses became a difficult and time-consuming chore for me. I told Karen we had to sell our house on Josephine Street and move to our land.

During that time, we still had the $5,000 we had planned to spend on our trip to Jordan, which we never took. While our house was for sale, we bought a double-wide and had it set on the east side of where I planned to build our house. I hired a company to install a septic tank and a drain field on the west side of the mobile home at a location adequate for our future home.

It was January 1970 when we moved into the mobile home. Although it was comfortable to live in, for months the roof leaked when it rained, and I had to get on the roof and caulk the joints.

One cool morning, I walked down to the barn to feed the horses, and there she was: our newborn filly. She had her mother's golden coat and some of her markings. I was ecstatic to see her attempting to climb the sawdust mound that I had in the corral, stumbling, falling, and getting up, over and over while Jeepers stood by calmly. We named the registered filly Kajian's Jipsy and called her Jipsy.

I read an article in a horse magazine on how to halter train a young colt or a filly. It didn't take long until she trusted me and did what she was asked to do.

When she was at an age ready for riding, I asked John McKay, a friend of Dave, to have her broken. John was a great guy, gentle with horses, and got a horse to obey him with no effort. When he brought her back, Jipsy was calm and receptive to being ridden.

I learned how to exercise Jipsy. The horsemen call it lunging. Holding the end of the long lead line that was attached to Jipsy's halter, I stood in the center of the corral, whip in hand, playing the role of a savvy horseman while she trotted in a circle around me.

As much as I loved horses, they had become an exhausting problem for me. And I knew if I didn't ride them often, they would be difficult to control. We sold Jipsy for a meager profit. Still, we had the other two horses to contend with. Horses were costly and took a lot of effort and care. And we were spending a lot of money on our land.

Hauling hay to the barn and unloading it was backbreaking work. Hay wasn't available in winter. A few ranchers, once they looked at us, didn't have qualms about selling us straw, which to us looked like hay. I still remember the time we were desperate to find hay. A woman who had a farm near us, sold us what she said had plenty of nutrition. "Just spill some molasses on it, and the horses will love it." Of course they did! I found out it was fine straw, not hay, and it was the molasses that the horses really loved.

I convinced Karen that we needed to get rid of our horses. She was disappointed, but since she didn't enjoy riding that much, she agreed it was the sensible thing to do. I decided to practically give them away.

I was done with my horseback riding craze. I concluded that as long as I was unable to relax riding a horse, I would never be a confident rider. It may have been my cowboy fantasy from reading Louis L'Amour and Zane Grey or my childhood memories of the Bedouin children riding bareback that instilled this fascination in me. Being around our horses (and to an extent training them) was an experience that I never regretted. I loved seeing our quarter horses, mother and filly, invigorated by a cool morning breeze, heads and tails up in a brisk run around our pasture, and I thought they were the most elegant living beings ever.

Once we got rid of our horses, I thought it might be wise to raise a calf on our land. It would eventually provide us with meat. We bought a day-old calf and hauled her in the back of our station wagon. To see the cute calf almost knocking us down while it sucked on a milk bottle was a pleasurable experience. The calf grew to be a heifer and it provided us beef in abundance—enough to make us want to become devout vegetarians.

After nine years of marriage, we planned to have children. Karen quit her teaching job, and in the fall of 1969, enrolled in a master's degree program at the University of Oregon.

Our first son, Kyle, was born on October 2, 1970, after a long day of labor. Holding Kyle in her arms, Karen had the widest smile ever. When I saw our newborn baby, my outlook on life changed. Our own child appearing in our lives seemed like a miracle. Later that night, when Karen and Kyle were still at the hospital, I sat on the couch alone in a daze, and the reality of being a father set in. Because of the hard labor, Kyle's face was almost flattened out of shape. Yet it didn't take long until he was the most beautiful baby with curly, blondish hair.

In the subsequent weeks, I woke up at night and bottle-fed Kyle while Karen rested. One day, as I lay on the recliner while he snoozed on my chest, I saw a mouse run up the curtain and crawl over the curtain rod. It freaked me out. Early in the morning, I looked all over to find mouse entry spaces. Under the heater, I found a sizable gap in the floor where mice came in and out as they pleased. Living in the mobile home served us well, but we experienced one problem after another.

While we lived in the mobile home, we ran out of storage space. So I built a small building just south of our mobile home, following a plan I found in a magazine. It had an old barn gable design and a concrete slab floor. I installed heat and light. It housed the hundreds of jars of fruits and vegetables that Karen canned. Later, we thought it might be a playhouse for Kyle, even though he had all the outdoors to roam and play as he wished, so we called it Kyle's House. We still called it that even once we transformed it for other purposes.

On October 22, 1972, our second son, Garrick, was born. I thought we wouldn't make it to the hospital in time and the baby would be born in the car.

Karen took a hiatus from her master's program to raise our two sons. Even with that demanding job, she applied her energy to tending our vegetable garden and orchard. She spent hours on her knees working in the garden, carrying Garrick in a baby carrier on her back while two-year-old Kyle played around as he pleased, often pulling green onions, his favorites, and chomping on them, dirt and all, like they were sweets.

In the southeast corner of our property, I planted strawberries. Karen froze bags of strawberries for our winter breakfasts. The food drier I had built using a lightbulb worked well for drying strawberries and other fruits and vegetables. The dried strawberries were some of our boys' favorite snacks, and they still talk about them. Drying gave the berries an intense flavor.

We bought a pregnant goat, and she had a female kid. We named the mother Muriel, and three-year-old Kyle decided to call the kid Little Muriel. She became Kyle's best friend, following him wherever he went. He would open the door of the mobile home and tell her, "No, Little Muriel, you can't come in." And of course, upon seeing the open door, she would trot right in.

We fed our boys goat's milk, and Karen made goat's milk yogurt and soft cheese. With an abundance of vegetables and fruit, meat, fresh goat milk, and yogurt in addition to the grains and sundries we bought from grocery stores, we were almost among the "live off the land" clan—self-sufficient.

When our boys were born, my responsibilities multiplied. Since I was the sole breadwinner, it was crucial that I keep my pharmacy job. My determination to build our house swelled. I was already thirty-nine years old, so I felt I had better do it sooner than later.

I was about to embark on a formidable job, and I hadn't thought of its gravity or even its feasibility, yet with steadfast enthusiasm and determination, I convinced myself I could do it—and I would, at all costs.

Building the barn, 1969

Building our house, 1973

CHAPTER 12

Our Home—The Ultimate Venture

For a guy like me who was not in optimum physical condition, who was mostly a dreamer (with more guts and stamina than sense), to embark on a heavy construction project seemed quite ambitious. I began to wonder if taking on such a formidable commitment might, in fact, be too crazy to even contemplate. Yet, I had the persistent conviction that whatever we could create on our land that might provide financial independence would be a valid pursuit. Building the house myself, without hiring a contractor, became the only plausible plan that would eliminate or reduce large monthly mortgage payments.

Karen and I found a floor plan for a cozy home and ordered a copy. The plan had three bedrooms, a living room, dining room, a small kitchen, and a double garage. We liked the general layout, but Karen preferred enlarging the kitchen and having it open to the combined living-dining room. So she redesigned the layout to her wishes. Since it was a significant modification, we had a local architect look at it. He approved the plan with minor changes. As soon as we had the blueprints, I applied for a building permit. It was early 1973.

The experience I had gained from building the barn was helpful, but building a house was much more involved than a simple rectangular barn. Framing, plumbing, and electrical work were complicated, and I needed to research how to do them. I drew diagrams of what I intended to do in my building project, and I acquired permits, always discussing my plans with the construction, plumbing, and electrical inspectors. It was essential I comply with the building code every step of the way.

By that point, Fred and I had been working for Valu-Mart drugstore for over four years, and all seemed to be going well with the company. Our working situation was tolerable, our twelve-hour-a-day work schedule was perfect for me with three or four days off each week to work on our house.

I hired someone to excavate the foundation area, set up the forms, and pour the concrete foundation. I ordered four-by-eight floor joists that were sixteen feet long. Once the concrete hardened, I began setting the heavy joists on the foundation at specified intervals to support the flooring—the first stage in building our house. It was a strenuous undertaking for one person.

Once I completed setting the floor joists, I was in a state of elation. Continuing with my building project not only made me tolerate my pharmacy work, but also made keeping it necessary. The day after I finished this first stage was Saturday, and I was at the pharmacy at eight thirty, feeling proud of my accomplishment, even though I had already spent much of our savings on the initial stages of my house-building project.

Around eight forty-five, I heard the store manager's voice on the loudspeaker. "All employees come to the snack bar right away." His voice was urgent, and it was an unusual request. His habit most mornings was to call a clerk or a floor supervisor to tend to something specific. He had never included all employees, even pharmacists.

Employees stood tense, not partaking in their usual morning chatter, while the manager and his assistant huddled, talking quietly together. Then their attention turned to us.

"I have bad news," the manager said. "Fred Meyer stores bought Valu-Mart, and they are converting this building into a storage warehouse." He told us we had one month to look for another job.

I couldn't believe what I'd heard. At that instant, I felt like the roof fell on my head.

I phoned Fred. He said he would be right down to find out what it was all about.

Should I call Karen, or wait until I get home? What to do? Have I made the stupidest mistake in my life, spending our savings on a project that I had no business undertaking, subjecting my family to a foolish notion?

There were only so many pharmacies in the Eugene and Springfield area. I was in no position to move to another state. If I considered selling our place, who in his right mind would want to buy it with a foundation that had no value to anyone but us? What if I couldn't find a job within the month?

"There is no reason to worry. We'll find another job," Fred said.

I was restless all afternoon, and since there wasn't much going on, I tried to occupy my time doing administrative work and wondering how to relay the bad news to Karen.

When I drove home that evening, upon seeing the welcoming smiles of my family, I felt a nagging pain in my chest. I told Karen what had transpired at the store. She listened but had little to say. I couldn't dismiss the guilt that overcame me for getting my family into this predicament.

I didn't have the will to go out and look at what I had already accomplished on my foolhardy project.

In my mind, I went over and over our dire situation but found no solution. If I couldn't find a pharmacy job, then I would have to take another job—but what? It was unlikely any business would hire me, knowing that as soon as I found a pharmacy opening, I would quit and leave them in a bind. It was clear that even though our boys were still little, Karen would have to get a teaching job.

Chaos at the pharmacy magnified with each hour. I was in a state of upheaval, trying my best to concentrate on filling prescriptions and answering phone calls as I was bombarded by customers who became aware of the news and wanted to find out how to transfer their prescriptions to another pharmacy.

And then I got an unexpected phone call. "I got a job at PayLess Drug Store at the Big M shopping center in Springfield," Fred said. "I mentioned you to the management, and they are receptive to your working here with me." A massive weight lifted off my chest. Thanks to Fred, I became an employee of PayLess Drug Store in Springfield.

Now that I was over the shock of losing my job so unexpectedly, and I was gainfully employed again, I wanted to continue my building work. But I needed money to proceed. I thought about borrowing money from our bank, the U.S. Bank in Junction City. I told the manager I needed to borrow $5,000. He asked me what it was for. I told him it was for home-building materials.

"Who is the builder?"

"I am."

"You're a pharmacist. You aren't a builder."

"No, I'm not."

"Many try to build their own houses and almost always give up," he said. "Then we end up taking over and undoing what they have done, and we are both losers."

He must have realized how disappointed I was. "Since you have a good job as a pharmacist, and you are in good standing with us, we can loan you a personal loan, but it would have nothing to do with building."

So I borrowed the $5,000 and ordered lumber and other materials. In a flash, that money disappeared. But I had the lumber and could proceed with the construction.

I framed the walls on the ground. Karen and I lifted the small wall sections on top of the sill and had them plumbed and braced. Jack and Bunny helped us raise the longer sections and brace and nail them together with the existing erected walls. It took two or three months to get the walls framed and secured with top plates.

We had always been thankful to have Jack and Bunny Huntley as our neighbors. We had collaborated and helped each other when needed. For months, we had problems with the submersible well pipe bursting. On such occasions, Jack came to the rescue. We ran a hose from Jack's outdoor faucets into our system for our household needs. I would call Jasper, and the two of us would pull out the heavy pipe from the 130-foot-deep well to find the rupture, which he would splice. And when Jack had a similar problem with his well, we reciprocated and came to his rescue.

The pipe bursting remained an aggravating problem for quite a while. I hired the Christensen Well Drilling company to solve the problem. When the man they sent pulled the pipe, he said it wasn't of the quality needed for that depth. He replaced it with a thicker pipe, and we've had no problems ever since.

With the wall framing done, I needed rafters to hold the roofing and tie the walls. I took the plans to a truss company. When they delivered the trusses, I was at the barn, feeding our livestock. The deliverymen asked Karen where the building crew was. "He's down at the barn feeding the chickens," she said.

I asked Jack to lend me a hand since it took two people to secure each end of the rafters to the walls. Once the rafters were erected, I'd wake up at daybreak to haul the half-inch exterior plywood sheets and nail them to the rafters. I had never been secure with heights, yet the will to do the job made me forget my phobia. Even though I have never been a physical person, my will to push on made me develop stamina.

After I framed the walls, installed the roofing, and erected the interior room partitions, I again ran out of money. While I tried to figure out how to get another loan and continue my work, I bought a pickup-load of rocks from a quarry and built four-foot-high stonework around the lower section of the front wall of the house. Although the work was decorative, it kept my enthusiasm and energy in the building project high without a break.

Because I had been paying large payments on my first

loan, it was somewhat easier to get another loan from the bank the next time I asked.

Installing the electrical and the plumbing came next. I studied several books on installing electrical wiring in houses. I faced a few complications. In the electrical work, I learned the hard way that I needed to stick with one brand of equipment. When I didn't, I had electrical failure. I also faced another problem. After I installed the bathtub's faucet and turned on the water, the faucet dripped in a weak stream. The first jarring conclusion that came to mind was that we had weak water pressure to the house and that we would have to live with the water shortage, not unlike what we had back at our home in Amman. I kept telling myself, "It's okay. It's a major disappointment, but I have no choice but to accept it." After all, American pioneers put up with worse conditions. When the plumbing inspector came by for his inspection, he complimented me on what I had done so far. I told him about the bathtub faucet. The trickle of water was all he could get too. He told me the faucet was defective. Replace it, and I wouldn't have any problem. I did, and it worked like a charm.

Soldering the joints of copper tubing as well as joining heating ducts in the crawl space was arduous, especially for one person doing the work.

I took it upon myself to make the kitchen cabinets, following a layout that Karen designed, as well as build floor-to-ceiling bookcases along one wall of the living room.

Throughout my house-building project I used only a handheld circular saw, whereas professional builders use a table saw that makes construction faster and much easier for precision work. But its use is difficult to master. Since I was done with owning guns and hunting, I traded my guns for a Sears radial arm saw, the second-best choice. Building the cabinets and bookcases needed precision tools, so I bought a router with attachments.

In the evenings after dinner, to practice using the radial arm saw, I made wood blocks for our boys. I trimmed a clear stock of two-by-fours into a variety of sizes to fit into a wagon that I built of plywood. It rolled on casters. On Christmas morning, I expected the cart with the blocks to be an exciting surprise for Kyle and Garrick, and I would take the credit. But to my surprise, there was a tag "From Santa" on it. Well, I couldn't argue with that. The boys loved the blocks and played with them for years and, of course, they figured out who Santa was. Later the cart and blocks were passed down to the grand-kids for more years of enjoyment.

When there was a lull in the building because of a material shortage, I took time to sew and stuff toy animals—gifts for our boys. I made a giraffe for Kyle and a kangaroo for Garrick. I learned to sew when I was four or five years old. My mother taught me how, as well as how to knit. When my sisters, all older than me, were at school, I watched my mother do her chores—dusting, cooking, knitting, mending socks, or sewing on her Singer sewing machine. While she did her household chores, I stayed out of her way. I didn't dream of doing anything that would upset her.

After finishing her chores, she would sit on the couch in the family room, with her right leg under her left and a bowl of vegetables in her lap. I often sat next to her and followed every move she made, snapping the ends of the green bean pods or peeling potatoes. Sometimes she would pick up her knitting needles and her colorful yarn to resume her knitting from the day before. I would sit mesmerized by the perpetual movement of the knitting needles as my sight followed the yarn going round and round over her slender index finger. She fixed her eyes on the tip of the pink needle as it went in and out, over and under, as if she were in a daze. The garment that lay on her lap would grow in length. On occasion, she would stop to examine her knitting. Sometimes she would pull the needle and unravel a line or two.

From my mother, I learned that it takes perseverance to perfect a skill that requires precision. And building the kitchen cabinets required both skill and precision. I used alder plywood for the sides of the cabinets and the floor-to-ceiling bookcases in the living room, and I used clear alder boards for trim. Using the router, I dowelled and glued joints that had a clean frontal finish. For the cabinet drawer joints, I used a tongue-and-groove system. Once the cabinets and bookcases were built, Karen and I stained them with mahogany stain then added a Varathane sealer.

In late 1974, we sold the mobile home and moved into our house.

In 1980, instead of using our two-car garage to store junk, we decided to turn it into a family room. It, too, would have a floor-to-ceiling bookcase the width of one wall. It would also house the six-foot Yamaha grand piano I bought for Karen for her upcoming fortieth birthday. The music store delivered the piano and placed it in front of the bookcase. And for a while this new room was also a warm place to do my watercolor paintings.

Three-year-old Kyle with his pet goat, Little Muriel

Celebrating Christmas in our unfinished house, 1973

Completed house, 1974

CHAPTER 13

Hopeful Enterprises

The Canary Venture

Throughout the years I spent in my pharmacy career, I searched for ways to grow or raise on our land what others might want or need to give us a reasonable income to support my painting practice. A few ventures turned out to be naive, and in retrospect, they often made little sense or were unproductive or even wasteful, yet they gave me hope I might be on the right track.

There was a time when breeders in Eugene and Portland sold canaries for fifty to one hundred dollars a bird. So why couldn't I breed canaries? Since childhood, birds had fascinated me—canaries in particular. I always wanted to have one or two in a cage to take care of, watch, and enjoy their songs. When I was thirteen, my sisters and I visited an old Greek man who lived on a hill in Amman. He had a few pine trees on his property and had hung cages with finches from them. He also had canaries in his home. He gave us a canary and a cage. We fed the canary cannabis seeds (*umbuz* in Arabic) that shops sold in burlap bags as bird food. We even enjoyed eating the roasted seeds ourselves.

During my enrollment at the UNM in Albuquerque, there was a year when I lived in an apartment, and my roommate was an Armenian student from Syria. We were having lunch one day when two narcotics agents appeared at the door. One of them carried a white bag with pistachio nuts addressed to my roommate that his parents had sent him from Syria. The other agent pulled a small envelope out of his pocket that had five seeds we recognized as umbuz seeds. "Do you know what these are?" The man asked. Sure, we knew. We told him they were seeds we fed birds and canaries. We even ate them ourselves. It appeared the narcotic agents had successfully germinated a few of the cannabis seeds they found in the bag. Seeing that we may have been two dumb boys, or else shrewd actors, or perhaps innocent, naive immigrants, they told my roommate to tell his parents not to send any pistachios or any other nuts again.

I researched housing, feeding, and breeding canaries and started breeding canaries in a big way. Kyle's House had heat and light, which made it perfect for this new ambition. I built wooden cages with wire fronts for the breeders and had floor-to-ceiling wire cages for a variety of finches. I studied books on breeding canaries and fed them millet, flaxseed, hulled oats, Nyjer, and other seeds and also added canthaxanthin to the water, which made the birds' plumes brilliant red. Because of their brilliant color, canary breeders called the breed by the fancy name "red factor canaries." I learned from books how to tag canaries for breeding records. I bought clips and a clip press and tagged each canary. Within a couple of years, I had over 100 canaries—but sold none.

At a certain point, as with my other enterprises, I decided I wasn't comfortable selling canaries, not for one hundred dollars apiece or for any price. I partitioned the building into two sections and let the canaries fly freely.

I always shut the glass windows, even though there was an inner screen. One day, to aerate the building, I opened the window. I assumed if I were to leave the aviary for an hour, the screen would keep away any predator in my absence. That day, I was late getting back to the canary building and found the screens torn and the canaries everywhere in the pasture. For days, I found them dead in the field.

Angler Worms

My canary fiasco didn't stop me from getting into another enterprise. In Oregon, many people fished for trout in our beautiful rivers and streams. I saw an advertisement in the paper on raising worms as bait for anglers. "A profitable enterprise," the ad said. I figured with all the space we had, why not try it? Maybe for a change, it would pay back. I hadn't thought exactly how it would turn into a profitable business or who would buy the worms. I did know the ground worms that were everywhere in our gardens were especially useful in enriching the vegetable garden. Breeders said that angler's worms weren't the same as ground worms. They sold a special pedigreed type of worm they called angler worms.

I phoned the lady who advertised them in the newspaper. Although the worms she showed me looked like common ground worms, she insisted they were different. I believed her. After all, she was the expert. "On the hook, they stay alive much longer," she said.

She showed me her bins of worms and told me about the elaborate compost and expensive peat moss I should use as bedding and that I should feed them cornmeal. She handed me an instruction page to follow for producing healthy worms. Among the pink worms in her bins, there were some white, tiny worms. When I asked her about those, she said they were babies. She sold me what she said was the breeding stock, a handful of worms in damp loam, and she assured me that in no time I would have a lucrative business. I later found out the white worms weren't babies; they were unwanted, pesky worms whose multiplying had to be discouraged at all costs, since they grew faster than the angler worms and ate a lot of the expensive cornmeal.

Instead of building one bin to grow them in, I built two. I figured I might as well get into it in a big way. In time, as had happened before, I decided it was too costly an effort, considering the money I was spending on cornmeal and peat moss. I didn't even know who would want to buy them. I gave up and dismantled the bins. But it wasn't a total loss; I spread the compost and worms in our garden.

Honeybees

Oregonians believed in protecting honeybees. Young and old agonized over their belief that insecticides killed the honeybees. GloryBee, a bee company, rented hives to clover farmers to pollinate their fields. Spring and summer, I saw stacks of hives in the corners of clover fields that were blanketed by white blossoms. The bees that fed on the clover blossoms produced clover honey. I figured I could grow bees, rent hives to farmers, and sell the honey. It seemed a bright idea. This venture had to be lucrative.

During those years, the GloryBee company was located in

a small building that had stacks of honeybee-growing equipment for bee growers. I bought a couple of ten-frame beehives, as well as protective gloves and a veil, a smoker, a syrup feeder, a book on beekeeping, and, of course, the bees.

I placed the hives along the back fence, away from our mobile home. Elated, I watched the bees happily getting in and out of the hives. It didn't take long until I was able to lift the cover and, using the smoker, handle the frames and observe the honey being formed. On TV, I saw a man handling the bees without gloves, so I got the courage to do the same. It was much easier to handle the frames without the bulky gloves. I got stung once or twice, and it was my fault. The man on TV said that even in a swarm, the bees are busy protecting the queen and are harmless. Someone could move the swarm with the queen into a new hive without getting stung or even disturbing the swarm. "Just scoop them into a box," the man said.

I found out that one of our neighbors was seriously allergic to bee stings. Being a good neighbor, I decided to end my bee-growing business.

A few years later, our boys and a couple of friends were playing in our backyard one day and came running to tell me about a swarm they saw on a tree branch close to where they were playing. Of course they wanted me to do something about it.

I remembered what the man on TV had said: "Bees, when swarming around their queen, do not cause a problem. One can scoop the entire swarm and place it in a box or a hive." I had gotten rid of all the bee equipment I had, but I figured

I'd do as the man on TV suggested. Carrying a cardboard box, I came close to the swarm. As soon as I touched the swarm, hundreds, maybe thousands, of bees came after me.

The boys stood far away, watching in horror as I waited it out. By luck, I wasn't seriously allergic to bee stings, yet my eyes and face swelled. Because I was the only pharmacist on duty that day, I had to go to work like that.

The Walnut Orchard

Still determined to make our place productive, I thought of planting an English walnut orchard so someday I could sell walnuts, which I assumed would turn into a profitable business. I ordered sixty bare-root walnut tree whips from another state. These trees were immune to a disease that in the past had destroyed quite a few English walnut tree groves in our area.

The date of their arrival was about six weeks out. In anticipation, I made a plan to plant them on our steep hill facing north. I measured and marked where I would plant the trees once they arrived. With pick and shovel, I began the exhausting work of digging, but a few of the holes, I hit limestone. For the roots to break through, the only thing I could do without abandoning the entire project was to crack the limestone with the pick to give the roots a chance to reach the soil beneath.

It took a few weeks to dig the holes. The trees arrived on time at the truck depot. They were an inch to two inches in diameter and around five feet tall. I staked the trees and covered them with the soil I had dug out. And I created a gorgeous walnut grove that we and the squirrels have enjoyed ever since.

CHAPTER 14

PayLess Drugs—An Impulsive Decision

The PayLess Drug Store was part of a chain with headquarters in Portland. Fred always said that the managers who ran the store had no managerial experience. Given a managerial badge by their higher ups, they felt grandiose. They had to wear suits and ties and work over sixty hours a week, with pay not much higher than the clerks. They resented the pharmacist pay scale, which was much higher, as well as the necessity of our presence in the drugstore at all times so the store could do business. To make themselves look good, the managers decided to cut payroll expenses. The only place they thought they could accomplish that was in the pharmacy department.

For months Fred and I worked without clerks, filling prescriptions, answering phone calls, as well as tending to customers at the register. Our computer system wasn't reliable. One problem after another paralyzed our workflow. If the computer system broke, problems piled up, and we faced disgruntled customers. During these moments, Fred was often on the verge of calling it quits. It came to the point when he couldn't stand it any longer. One morning he had an argument with the manager and just walked out, leaving the pharmacy unattended.

We had been working for PayLess for over ten years. I had been an unhappy pharmacist in the best of times and had been at the end of my patience with my pharmacy career for quite a while. In this unprecedented situation, I had to decide what was best for me.

In those years, Kyle was in kindergarten and Garrick was in day care. Karen had gone back to work after a five-year hiatus. While we were both at work, Karen's friends, who had children our boys' ages, took care of Kyle and Garrick after school until one of us picked them up.

I phoned Karen when she got home from school to tell her about what had happened at the store, and that I was thinking of quitting as well.

"Do it. It's time to do what you've always wanted to do," she said.

Soon after I quit working at PayLess, their bookkeepers sent me a note informing me I had $30,000 invested in PayLess stocks. It was a pension that they owed me. I learned I could roll the money over into IRA mutual funds with no penalty, so I did.

I had been thrashing around in my attempts to learn the craft of painting for a few years, yet in no way had I reached the status of an accomplished painter, let alone gained the status of an artist. In quitting the pharmacy, I found myself in a position where I would have to prove that I was a committed painter and not a hobbyist.

When Aleece and Vahan immigrated to the United States, they lived among an Armenian community in New York in the same apartment complex where Vahan's brother Victor and his family lived. They were employed by Mays department store in New York and were content with their new lives. They had visited us twice and especially loved the temperate climate and the serenity of life where we lived.

In 1976, Vahan had open heart surgery. Because Oregon had a milder climate than New York, they decided to move to Oregon and live in an apartment close to us. They thought it would speed up his recovery. We suggested they live with us for a while to be sure they liked it here before they made a permanent move.

It didn't take long until Vahan was outdoors wearing his bright blue short-sleeve T-shirt and puttering around in the garden, watering plants, and weeding. It was what he needed—a life far from being cooped up in an apartment in a big city. I was thrilled to see him happy.

At one point, an idea came to me. What if I built an apartment for them in the spot where we had parked our mobile home? It would have the underground plumbing already installed in that spot. The building would have a bathroom, a bedroom, a small kitchen, and a living room. They would have their own private little space close to yet independent of us. And no rent expenditure! Initially, they thought it was a perfect idea.

I became excited about the project. I set up the concrete forms and had a cement company pour the floor slab and another company deliver the lumber, then I was ready to start the framing.

While it thrilled Vahan to be here, Aleece, unknown to us, was unhappy, feeling lonely and missing her Armenian friends in New York—just as I was about to frame their apartment. The more she thought about it, the lonelier she became. She would stay in her room and weep. I still worked at PayLess at the time and was very unhappy myself. Learning of her unhappiness didn't help mine. While Vahan spent his time outdoors, Aleece was by herself with nothing to do.

Because her loneliness was unbearable, they moved back to the Armenian neighborhood in New York to be with Vahan's brother and family and their Armenian friends.

Now I had to deal with the concrete slab on which I had intended to build the apartment—and all the building materials that had already been delivered.

For the next few weeks, I framed the structure with windows facing north, west, and south, according to my initial plans. I had the rafters in place and plywood sheathing, roofing, and siding similar to what I had used in our house. Once the apartment was weatherproofed, we used it as a wood storage building.

All along, I painted in the family room or outdoors. In 1986, I partitioned the building according to the original apartment plan. I did the electrical and plumbing, then I drywalled the walls and the ceiling. I installed bathroom plumbing, a toilet, and a sink, and hooked up the electricity to provide heat and lighting. I built shelves to store my large paintings and other shelves for my watercolor supplies. The woodshed turned into a comfortable painting studio.

When Vahan passed on, Aleece came to visit us and stayed for about a month. We had already turned the garage into a family room with a bed and a couch. And that's where she slept and loved it. And at this time she was happy puttering in the garden, picking fruit, cooking Armenian meals, and having a good time. By then, I had already quit PayLess Drug Store. Although I needed to spend my time painting, I still kept my sister company, chatting and watching *Rockford Files* on TV.

During her visit, I even painted a portrait of her in acrylic in the Fauves style. It was colorful and wild; she loved it. Then she moved to California and rented a small apartment in the Palisades and got a job as a seamstress. She did very well, making alterations, including some for a few demanding movie stars. She had Armenian friends living in her neighborhood, and for a while, she was content with her life.

At some point work became difficult for Aleece, so my youngest sister, Alexandra, asked Aleece to live with her and her second husband, George, in Philadelphia. When George passed on several years later, Alexandra and Aleece moved to Texas until eventually they both went back to New York. Aleece had become afflicted with dementia. It became difficult for Alexandra to take care of her, so she found a pleasant care facility for her where they treated her well and she was happy. In 2019, Aleece passed on peacefully. Alexandra mailed me her ashes. Since my sister loved to spend time in the garden picking vegetables and apples, what better place to sprinkle her ashes than under an apple tree?

CHAPTER 15

Aspiration

In the months after I quit PayLess Drug Store, painting made me the happiest I had ever been. I took a couple of watercolor workshops from the Watercolor Society of Oregon's visiting artists, yet still relied on the art books I had collected. I painted two to three paintings a day to learn the craft as quickly as I could. Within a few months, I developed the ability to paint pictures that some admired, and a few even purchased. The first painting I sold was a watercolor landscape that a friend bought.

Painters in Eugene showed their work in restaurants and banks. I framed a few of my best paintings that I believed were suitable for public viewing. And despite my introverted personality and reluctance to market my artwork, I concluded I had no choice but to seek outlets that would display my works. I approached a U.S. Bank in Eugene and showed them photos of my art. Impressed, they scheduled a day to hang my paintings. The morning I hung my paintings at the bank, I was anxious, wondering what the people who passed by me thought of them.

I approached the Beaverton Arts Commission, which showed artwork of Portland and Beaverton artists in local businesses on a monthly rotation. I became one of their artists.

I also joined a company that provided artists an opportunity to display and sell their works in major city malls. My first experience with this company was exhibiting at a mall in Coos Bay, Oregon. I packed my framed paintings in my Datsun station wagon, drove 110 miles to the Coos Bay mall, and set up my display in my assigned spot. Because I couldn't afford to spend nights in a motel, for the two days of the mall exhibition, after closing at 9 p.m., I drove back on the winding narrow road, then returned to my post at the mall the next morning. In this venture, the only benefit I gained was to meet a few painters and a few sculptors. For the two days, none of us did well. A few people passing by gave us a casual look—others, not even a glance. It was a tortuous and demoralizing experience.

At the Washington Square mall show in Portland, I sold two paintings to a physician's wife. I was thrilled, even though I spent more on my motel room than what I got for the sale of the paintings. Still, I was ecstatic that a stranger wanted my artwork and was willing to pay for it. I felt the need to not only send her a thank you note but also to gift her a small watercolor.

During those years, all my work was experimental, and I took none of it as precious art. In my mind, there was always the intent to do better work. But I didn't have a clue as to what "better" really meant. Once in a while, I got the feeling that what was happening on my paper or canvas was something new, fresh, or exciting. It may have been a brushstroke that I applied accidentally or many brushstrokes that showed a vigorous, crusty texture, or maybe a thick black line or a passage of color, or a combination of colors that appealed to me. A few of my paintings would turn out to my liking and many wouldn't. Often, at the end of the day, I had to discard what I had been working on all day long. Yet I never felt discouraged. It was more of a relief to begin anew early morning the next day. I placed inexhaustible energy into painting week after week.

At Maude Kerns Art Center, I gained the ability to work from a model, creating reasonably good watercolor portraits in the three-hour sessions. I developed the ability to apply juicy, decisive, and vigorous brushstrokes. It wasn't easy to paint the figure of a model on a large watercolor paper in three hours. It demands initial accurate drawing to achieve a good composition and then decisiveness in applying the paint. Watercolor applied deftly without overworking it, when successful, resulted in a work that had sparkle and not a dull look. I took risks, striving for bold and intense pictures, not the washed-out watercolors commonly seen when glazing is used. Glazing is a common process in watercolor painting. Once the painting dries, one paints another transparent coat over it, either to darken it or change the color. The glazing often dulls the painting. When painted decisively, in one go, as I did, without glazing, the painting is fresh and sparkles. Although the figure painting session may have been a mentally and physically exhausting activity, at the end of each three-hour session, I felt more energized than ever.

Week after week, I developed the technical ability to create art that other artists admired, which was the most cherished reward for me. A renowned Oregon acrylic artist, Satsuko Hamilton, exchanged one of her large landscapes for one of my watercolor portraits. Satsuko and her inspiring watercolor-artist husband, George Hamilton, were the most admired and emulated artists in Oregon. Their encouragement and appreciation of my paintings was the satisfaction I treasured more than seeking the appreciation of the public.

George and Satsuko had enough confidence in my work to recommend me to the prestigious Rental Sales Gallery of the Portland Art Museum, and I became a member. The gallery sold and rented paintings of their artists. Twice a year, I submitted work to be juried by the gallery. The gallery accepted most and rented or sold a number of them.

George and Satsuko also referred me to a gallery in a small shopping center, a location a few miles south of Portland. I applied and got accepted.

At Maude Kerns, I managed the open studio painting and drawing sessions. In the painting sessions, we had one three-hour pose. In the drawing session, I used various media such as pencil, charcoal, watercolor, India ink, color inks, and watercolor crayons. We began with short, two-minute gestural exercises before moving on to five-, fifteen-, and sixty-minute poses. During the final pose, I painted a watercolor.

On days I wasn't doing my art at Maude Kerns, I painted on my own. I painted plein air landscapes and still-life paintings from outdoor setups or did still-life paintings in my studio.

I practiced diligently my primary medium, watercolor, and attained the technical ability to become a member in the prestigious Watercolor Society of Oregon—a turning point in my artistic career and a boost to my confidence. I entered a few of their yearly shows that were juried by prominent watercolor artists of Oregon and California. A few paintings I submitted didn't get in, but many did, which gave me tremendous energy and assurance. The rejections made me accept the difficulties in an artist's career. I learned that although the jurors' task was to focus on outstanding quality of work regardless of style or subject, one couldn't disregard the personal likes and dislikes of the juror. When, at a later date, I juried a few shows myself, I understood the challenges jurors face.

In a surprise turn in my artistic achievements, I received the sweepstake award for the watercolor *David*, a portrait I did of a live model at Maude Kerns Art Center. It was juried by the renowned California watercolor artist, Milford Zornes.

The Watercolor Society of Oregon invited me to do demos for their members during two of their conventions. One was held in Eugene and another in Portland. It was an honor, since I had switched my primary medium from watercolor to oil and no longer took part in their shows.

While I had stopped painting large watercolors intended for shows, I still maintained the almost daily habit of doing small sketches in watercolor—an activity I never tired of doing. I called these sketches "diaries in pictures."

CHAPTER 16

Sergei Bongart

In 1984, I saw an article in an issue of *Southwest Art* magazine on the Russian artist Sergei Bongart. There was a spread of dazzling images of some of his paintings. I was instantly awed by what I saw. Each mesmerizing image opened my eyes to the power of art. I read and reread the story of the artist. I learned that he had a school in Los Angeles. He spent half the year there, teaching and painting, and the other half at his home and studio in Rexburg, Idaho, where he conducted spring and summer workshops.

The discovery was like a talisman that would shape my own world. I knew what I needed to do.

I talked it over with Karen and sent my deposit for a week-long workshop in Rexburg. I received pamphlets with more images of Bongart's paintings and a few images of the work of his student instructors, Sunny Apinchapong and Ron Lukas. The information I received also noted that painters using any medium were welcome.

I was in heaven. I packed my VW bus, the one we called the hippie bus since it had many wild designs all over it, and I headed to Rexburg with my watercolor supplies and equipment.

Sergei Bongart, a showman with a dynamic personality, had emigrated penniless from Ukraine to the US. He had the talent to befriend the rich, among which were notable actors such as James Cagney, Jack Lemmon, and Gene Hackman. The latter two became his students. In no time, Bongart became a powerful entity as an artist. He not only had a commanding personality but also a savvy business aptitude. His dashing image as an eccentric, first-class artist separated him and his impressive artwork from other artists, placing him in a unique position in the California art world. His paintings and drawings stood above and beyond what I had seen. Garnering that forceful impression of the artist and his work gave me an inkling as to which path I needed to pursue.

I arrived in Rexburg and went to the complex of apartments with a courtyard where we were to live and have the introduction to the workshop. There were at least sixty students who came from all over the United States, Europe, the Middle East, and some other foreign countries. All were inspired to spend a week or two lost in art, hoping that time might change or enrich their artistic lives. Although being among the many student artists in the class may have inspired me, I wondered how I would fit in among these men and women, some of whom had already studied with him for a few years. He gave scholarships to young promising students who attended his LA school, and some of them were present in Rexburg.

From the first day, I was in a dreamlike atmosphere. I was assigned a room with a kitchenette. I got situated and waited until the evening hour when we would meet the master and I would be among the throng of participants.

Even in the informal evening gathering, he had a captivating personality. With a thick accent, he spoke in generalities about what the workshop entailed and chatted amicably, welcoming back the students who had been studying with Bongart for years. Many students congregated around him. I felt lost among them. I stood back, taking in all the hype and enthusiasm.

In the morning, in an expectant, emotionally charged atmosphere, we sat on metal chairs lined up in rows in an expansive barn-like structure, waiting. Morning sun rays streaked in, finding their way through the cracks in the galvanized siding. In the middle, on a raised platform, sat Bongart's girlfriend, Patricia La Grande. His student instructors had placed a thirty-by-forty-inch canvas on Bongart's massive easel. On a card table in front of the easel was his twenty-four-by-thirty-inch palette with dazzling mounds of oil paint like a rainbow around its periphery—cadmium yellow (pale and dark), cadmium red light, alizarin crimson, ultramarine blue, phthalo blue, cerulean blue, viridian, dioxazine purple, yellow ochre, burnt sienna, burnt umber, ivory black—and a full pound of flake white paint next to a glass cup filled with the honey-like Grumbacher paint medium, and a pot of turpentine for cleaning brushes. On a table, behind the easel, was an uninspiring still-life setup of a pot, a bottle, and other items on a dusty tan cloth. On the left corner were a couple of easels with Patricia La Grande's figurative paintings.

We awaited Bongart's arrival for what seemed like over an hour in suspenseful silence, only hearing occasional whispers between friends.

I looked at all the fascinating artwork on the walls—still life, portrait, and landscape paintings and drawings of the artist-student instructors, Sunny Apinchapong and Ron Lukas. I wondered if I would ever paint like that. At that moment, I had a determination embedded within me that it was possible, and I would be the one to make it happen.

The galvanized barn gate behind us groaned. All heads turned back to look. Bongart entered, wearing Cossack-style high boots and horseman's trousers. As in a funeral march, he walked down the aisle, looking straight ahead. He tipped his head to the side with a faint smile, acknowledging his girl-friend, and resumed his walk toward his easel. He picked up a brush, held it like a conductor's baton, walked to the center of the room, and faced us.

"Hello, everybody." His deep voice, with a Russian accent, resonated in the hushed room.

They had told us it was acceptable to record him and even take photos during his demonstrations. We were prohibited from talking or asking questions until he took a break. Then he welcomed questions.

After standing silent for a minute, scanning the audience left to right, he began speaking. He told us that there are two ways of painting: coloring and painting as an artist. In coloring, we look at the subject and pick the color we think we recognize and paint it on our canvas. When painting as artists, on the other hand, we see the nuances in color, comparing the local colors of similar hues, red to red, green to green, and so on. If we are looking at all the reds in a still-life setup, for instance, we need to compare the temperature of all the reds, how cool and how warm each is in relation to one another. What causes the nuances in hues is the effect of the environment the subject is in. If we look at white it is never "tube" white. The white in a still life is affected by what's next to it. If there's a red apple on the white tablecloth, the white close to the apple turns reddish white. As artists we also compare values, dark to dark and light to light. When we apply this information to our canvas, the paintings will shimmer, and colors will vibrate.

There is an abstraction beneath every good painting, no matter what style one prefers. Bongart said that, although Andrew Wyeth painted every blade of grass, there was an extraordinary, simple overall design, an abstract form, beneath all his detailed work.

Bongart said we should paint in stages: first, the block-in—placement of the subject on the canvas in a pleasing form with a thin wash of ivory black and phthalo blue—second, applying cool and warm spots of color, comparing similar hues. This second stage should be in the middle value and should comprise about 90 percent of the painting time. In the last 10 percent, the darkest darks and the lightest lights are added. And with a few accents, the painting is completed. When painting outdoors, he added, always use an umbrella so you can see color.

He went to his easel and looked at the still-life setup for a while. He covered the white canvas with a transparent gray mixture of a soupy black and phthalo blue, then, with the same mixture but thicker paint, in a loose manner drew the simplest form of the still life by working all over the canvas. Next, he applied a transparent wash, comparing values, dark to dark and light to light, of what he detected in the setup.

The focus on colors came after. Again, he compared similar hues and nuances, cool to cool and warm to warm. He finally sprinkled a few accents here and there. With a mesmerizing transformation and invigorating freshness, the painting sparkled and had a life of its own, portraying the essence of the still life. As soon as his demonstration was over and after a thunderous applause, he answered a few questions, then left.

In the large classroom, the instructors had still-life setups all around the barn. Students scattered to have their lunch. Not to waste time, I ate my sandwich, then clipped an Arches Cold Press sheet of watercolor paper to a stiff backing and laid it on the dirt floor of the barn. I sat on a canvas stool and began to paint a watercolor of one of the still-life setups.

I had completed my still life but still needed a few accents when I realized a figure was standing behind me. I looked up. Bongart was watching me. I stood up. He looked at my painting for a little while and then at the still-life setup. "Goot," he said in his thick Russian accent. To get that compliment so early in the workshop from the master was a major lift to my confidence.

"Do you want to become an artist?" he asked.

"Yes," I said.

"In the morning, the art supply store brings art supplies. Buy oil painting stuff, and paint oil." And he told me what to buy—a few oil paint colors, a few canvases, two or three brushes, a palette, and a few other items.

He suggested I should paint in oils, and if I mastered the oil medium, I could paint in any other medium easily.

Early the next morning, the art store representative

brought art supplies and canvases and spread them out on a table. I stocked up on oil paint, a dozen canvases in the sizes Bongart recommended, brushes, Grumbacher medium and turpentine, and a plastic palette. I intended to follow his advice.

Next to the large classroom, there was another room that wasn't as large but had enough space for a dozen students. At the center, there was a high stand and a chair for a model. Most of the students in the workshop preferred to paint still lifes and landscapes. I concentrated on painting figures and landscapes in the oil medium but also continued doing watercolor still-life paintings during my lunch hour.

At night, we were painting a man who sat on a chair in the middle of the small classroom. Crowded with our easels, one next to the other, we began painting the figure. A woman in her fifties stood next to me. She had already started her painting while I was still trying to block the figure on my canvas with a phthalo blue and ivory black mixture. Bongart showed up and walked around with a stick in his hand. When he came up to the woman next to me, who seemed confident in the way she applied her brushstrokes, he stopped, looked at her canvas, then said, "Go out to the other room and paint still life for the next week." She spun around to face him, fuming, her face drained with anger. "I have been a portrait painter for the last twenty-five years, and you tell me to go out there and paint still life?"

"Okay," he said with a shrug, and walked past her. He looked at what I was doing, took the brush from my hand and mixed the black with a stiffer paint than what I was using and said I would have more control with stiffer paint. Putting the tip of the brush on the canvas, he drew a perfect line and handed the brush back to me.

The artist next to me bundled her painting tools and canvas and left the classroom. As I remember, she painted still life for the workshop duration, as he had suggested.

I heard he had told a student to forget about painting and take up needlework instead. I also heard that when someone asked him why he was so harsh with a few of his students, he said that if these people were committed to be artists, they wouldn't listen to him and would keep on painting regardless of what he said. But if their heart wasn't in painting, why struggle to do something that they weren't interested in? Why not take up something fun, a hobby they would enjoy?

During the workshop, I befriended a German student, Guido Frick. He loved the US and loved to listen to country-western music. He visited me in my room, and sometimes we went for lunch at a restaurant and chatted about our mutual passion for painting. In Germany, he had studied with a renowned Czech artist. Even though Guido was an advanced oil painter, he knew he would benefit a lot from attending Bongart's workshops.

One time, when Guido came to my room, he heard the country-western music I was listening to on my transistor radio, and he ran back to his room and returned with his own radio to tune it to the same station.

In my room, I did a watercolor portrait of Guido. The portrait came out okay, colorful for a watercolor. Later on, in the barn classroom, I had it set along a wall with a mat around it, beside other students' paintings. When Bongart came by and he saw the watercolor of Guido, he said, "Guido!" as if surprised.

On the third day of the workshop, Bongart painted a Russian peasant woman from artist Malyavin's figure pencil sketch. Bongart admired Malyavin among other notable Russian artists, such as Repin.

Bongart clipped the reproduction of Malyavin's sketch on the side of the easel next to his canvas. With fresh mounds of paint on his palette, he began his painting in the same process as he had done with his still life—with the same color combinations, blocking in the figure on his canvas. He drew a gorgeous Russian peasant woman with the black mixture of phthalo blue and ivory black. Had he left it at that stage, it would have been a striking sketch, exquisite on its own. But he soon applied color with abandon with big brushes. On his canvas, the woman's image stood against a background of a green Russian countryside. Her face had a lovely glow. She wore a blue smock and a shawl with vivid orange and red flowers. With a few touches here and there, he finished the demo. It was a superb figurative masterpiece.

Outdoors, our model, a blonde woman in a yellow dress, sat on a chair under a parasol while every one of us in the group who painted the figure lined up in a half circle facing the model. Each of us had an umbrella above us. I finished a lighthearted, high-key portrait of the model that I still enjoy looking at to this day.

In his third demo, Bongart painted a stormy landscape from one of his small pencil sketches. Dark washes dripped all over the canvas interspersed with spots of drier brushstrokes. Awed, we watched the canvas turn into a stormy sky with ominous clouds.

In the afternoon, we scattered all over the countryside. Bongart had told us that to paint like an artist, we needed to train ourselves to see nuances in color in nature and apply that knowledge to the canvas. The only way to see those nuances was through painting outdoors. Photos would never give us the true color found in nature. Student artists in Russian art academies, during five years of study, drew from classic sculptures, painted from live models, and, for three months a year, painted landscapes outdoors. Once the student artist painted outdoors for a period and understood the importance of seeing the nuances in nature, then he or she could translate this knowledge into studio work even if he or she were to paint from sketches or from imagination. What I understood Bongart to say was that painting plein air (outdoor painting) was a necessary learning experience to see nuances in color. Even accomplished studio artists needed to paint plein air once in a while to be reminded of the nuances in nature so they wouldn't get into bad habits and forget how to make an exciting painting.

Bongart also told us that when we were painting on canvas, we needed to be sure to scrape any tired-looking segments, then repaint. It would give the painting a patina, a quality superior to painting it in one go.

I was painting at a park as all the students scattered around in their chosen areas. In the middle of the painting, somewhat happy with my progress, a couple of women came over to give me compliments. In the distance, I saw Bongart coming our way. I told the women that the man was our instructor. They said he would like what I have done. He came over as the women stepped back. He looked at it for a while, then he said, "Scrape," and left. I scraped the whole painting while the women watched in puzzlement.

I continued with the painting. Later on, Bongart came over again, and again he said, "Scrape." But this time, he gave me a few pointers to keep in mind.

Many years later, I understood it was the common work habit of Russian painters to scrape and paint, over and over, in order to build up a beautiful patina that the artist cannot get when completing the painting alla prima, or finishing the painting in a single application rather than multiple layers.

On the last day of the workshop, Bongart invited us to visit his studio late in the evening. Until then, we hadn't dared even come close to investigate his house or his studio setting.

His gallery room accommodated twelve students at a time. While those twelve students were inside, the rest of us stood outside, waiting in line in the freezing cold. My teeth were chattering. I thought it was cruel to make us stand there in the freezing outdoors for over an hour. When it was our turn to go in, we witnessed the most dazzling exhibition. Some paintings were hung on the walls, others on easels, and a few were propped along the base of the walls. On an easel was his painting *The Armenian*. I loved that painting so much and asked Patricia La Grande how much it cost. Of course, the price was a steep $6,000 that I couldn't afford—and that was in 1983.

During the workshop, I had befriended Natasha, a blonde

Russian artist. She suggested we visit the Berberians, two Armenian brothers who had emigrated from Russia. The older brother, Ovanes, was an accomplished painter who had studied painting in Russia before emigrating to the US. The younger brother, Galust, was still a beginner. I drove Natasha to visit the brothers. We found them painting along a stream. They were pleased to see us, and they said they had finished painting and would love to have us visit their home.

It was an immense building with no furniture. Ovanes had an extensive still life set up on a low table with his painting easel close by with a half-finished painting of the still life. He was a meticulous painter, colorful, and bold in the Russian style, although his work was not as loose as Bongart's. Years later, when I visited galleries in New Mexico, I found his paintings priced at $20,000. He had become well known throughout the West and Midwest. Galust was a delightful young man. He brought out a dozen or more of his small plein air paintings and placed them against the walls of the huge vacant room for us to view. I thought they were beautiful unfinished and fresh sketches, much looser than his brother's. Ovanes showed me a portfolio of his nude figurative pencil sketches. He was proud of his drawings. I liked them, but they weren't special. His still-life paintings were very complicated and had an overly finished look unlike many Russian contemporary painters'. Yet they were superb pieces of art.

A few years later, my family and I were at the Frye Art Museum in Seattle. The Berberian brothers were sitting on a bench by the entrance. They were pleased to see me, and I, too, was delighted to see them. Ovanes asked me to help him fill out an application to be represented in the museum. The brothers wanted me to go paint with them at the harbor, but I couldn't as Karen and our boys were with me.

Later, I heard that the brothers went their separate ways. Ovanes became a very successful and sought-after artist. Galust also became accomplished, but he was a recluse. When I saw images of his work, I liked them more than Ovanes'. Although a few galleries represented him, he remained out of the limelight. No one knows much about him, and it's difficult to find his work on the internet. Ovanes attained considerable success. He bought a large home in Rexburg on a piece of land where he has yearly workshops similar to Bongart's. I saw photos of his workshop posted online by one of his students. He had outdoor still-life setups for students placed around his enormous property as well as many umbrellas for students to use.

When I drove home after Bongart's workshop, I felt as if I had been in a dream for a week. I was exhausted but inspired and determined to follow this new, exciting path. What had been impressed on me wasn't what I learned in technical knowledge of the craft so much as Bongart's philosophy on art and what it takes to become an artist—a philosophy I already believed. To be an artist is a way of life that shapes one's existence.

Touched by what I saw in Bongart's paintings, I vowed that a day would come when my paintings would have that boldness and possess the power of color to inspire other student artists, as his work had done for me. Whenever I had free time, I painted in oils, outdoors (rain or shine) or in my studio. I was in a battle against time, determined to succeed no matter what.

Although after Bongart's workshop, oil had become my primary medium, watercolor still remained my favorite for sketching.

Now in the open studio at Maude Kerns, I did forty-by-thirty-two-inch oil portraits instead of watercolor. I worked fast with large brushes and applied paint intuitively, with an exactitude that portrayed not only a semblance of the model but also the character of the model. My paintings still retained the unfinished look that I sought for in all my work and what I believed was the essence of Bongart's fantastic work that attracted me.

Some of my initial attempts weren't successful, and I would scrape them off and spend a lot of time cleaning the surface as best I could, which took more time than the painting itself in order to save the canvas. My failures didn't affect my motivation to keep on painting and experimenting. Off and on, I tried to emulate many styles of painting, yet I realized most styles weren't something I would want to do day in and day out. Soon, I concluded that the best path to follow was to free myself from any preconceived process. Painting a lot and painting fast, a process that didn't allow time to think or plan, relied on an intuitive approach. Most of my paintings were sketchy or gestural, a style that appealed to me. My temperament didn't allow for spending a lot of time on a painting. I would soon lose interest, and the painting would start on a downward spiral.

CHAPTER 17

Art Galleries and Trust

Galleries intimidated me, even as a visitor. Their directors presented themselves as experts on art, and I hadn't gained the courage and confidence to present myself as an artist.

When I came home one day after spending the morning painting at Hendricks Park in Eugene, my son Kyle said that I had received a call from the Franklin Gallery in Portland, and the director was interested in representing me. He'd given Kyle the gallery's phone number.

Only a few months earlier, I had received a surprise letter from a gallery in Boca Raton, Florida. The director had said she was impressed by my work and wanted to represent me in her gallery. It's an honor when a gallery approaches an artist for representation. It instantly provides validity to the artist's work. I sent her slides of a few of my oil paintings. She and the gallery owner commended my work, and I shipped the paintings they had chosen. Not long after, I received a letter that the gallery was closing, and the owner wondered if he could buy the paintings at a discount instead of shipping them back. Even though it was disappointing news, I thought it was a good deal. They paid me what I expected, which gave me some confidence in the gallery's professional ethics.

Now the Portland gallery wanted to represent me, another important development in my artistic career. When I phoned the gallerist, he said he had a good relationship with the Beaverton Art Commission, had seen my paintings shown in their roaming exhibits, and would like to represent me in his gallery. He asked that I bring him at least eight of my best work.

I drove to Portland with eight of my best paintings and arrived at the gallery a few minutes after the morning opening hour. The doors were still closed.

Shortly after, a man parked his red convertible in front of the building and introduced himself as the director and welcomed me to the gallery. He assisted me in bringing in my large watercolor paintings and we placed them against a wall.

I had never been in the gallery, so I looked around at what he had—a lot of Dalí prints and prints of other artists I wasn't familiar with, as well as a few small original paintings. *My paintings will stand out here,* I thought, since I didn't see any other work like mine.

He studied my paintings for a time, giving me the impression of a guy who could appraise good art. He stressed his good relationship with the Beaverton Art Commission as an invited speaker.

He praised my artwork and told me he had some clients already interested in my work, and he would phone them right away. "I will let you know how it goes," he said. He gave me a receipt. I thanked him and drove home, enthused that he implied I might already have a sale of one of my paintings.

A week passed, then another, and another, and for a month I didn't hear from him. I decided to give him a call just to keep in touch. The phone rang and rang. No answer. I called the next day and the next. After about a week, the gallery phone line was disconnected. Faced with a perplexing situation, I phoned the Beaverton Art Commission asking them if they knew the director of the gallery. They said yes, they did, and yes, he had a good relationship with them. They said they would check on it themselves and call me back.

It turned out that they had no more information than I did. I asked an artist friend in Portland if he was in town to drive by the gallery and let me know what he found. He said the gallery was out of business and that he looked through the windows and there were no paintings.

I drove to Portland and talked to the owner of the store next to the gallery to find out what he knew about it. The man said that the gallery had gone out of business a month earlier, but he had a key and could let me in to see if I could find my paintings. There was no artwork—nothing except for trash strewn all over the floor.

The Watercolor Society of Oregon newsletter mentioned a lawyer who represented artists. I phoned him. The man said it would cost me $6,000 to look in to the matter as he needed to hire someone to look for the owner. If I knew his whereabouts myself, the lawyer could do something about it, but it would still cost a lot of money.

I decided it might be wise to inform the authorities about my situation. I drove to Portland once again, phoned the police station, and stated my problem. They said they would have officers meet me at the entrance of the Portland Library. Two police officers showed up and asked me a few questions. People who were entering and exiting the library looked at me askance while the officers took notes. This put me in an uncomfortable position, thinking whoever passed by probably assumed I had done something wrong.

When I told the officers that the gallery was out of business and I did not know the owner's whereabouts, they said they would look in to it—I haven't heard from them since.

I stewed over this for a year, feeling helpless. Even the authorities didn't consider an artist's work important. At a certain point, I convinced myself that if the guy thought my paintings were valuable enough to commit a crime, I should be okay and forget about it. Over time, I put it out of my mind, except for the occasional momentary irritating memory of my helplessness as an artist.

CHAPTER 18

Roving Pharmacist

For over a year, I painted two to three paintings daily in my struggle to attain my goal. Yet I still questioned whether it was conceivable to make a living as a painter. Guilt of inadequacy weighed on me.

The management of our finances was solely my responsibility since Karen had a demanding teaching career and didn't pay attention to them. I had neglected them for a while as I was absorbed by my artistic demands. The art supplies I ordered, even if from discount art supply stores, were costly. I believed that to be successful as a painter I needed to paint a lot and not worry about how much paint I used. Often, by the end of the day when I had an unsuccessful oil painting, I would scrape off all the expensive paint in order to reuse the canvas.

A major problem surfaced one day when I phoned Jerry's Artarama, a discount art supply store, to order a few tubes of paint. The saleswoman took my order and my Visa number and put me on hold to verify my credit card status. When she came back on the line, she asked if I had another credit card to use as the one I had given her hadn't gone through. I said I didn't and to please try again. She returned with the same response. *There must be some mistake,* I thought. I hung up and phoned my Visa provider and got the shocking news that we had exceeded the $5,000 credit limit. Shaken, I cut the card in half.

Taking a good look at our finances, I realized we'd been behaving as if we still had two paychecks, not one, and my exorbitant art expenses added to the problem. I immediately took a part-time job with a pharmacist-on-call group. When they needed me, they would call me. Even if the hours were sporadic, the income from the job would take financial pressure off us. To my surprise, they called me to work more times than I imagined.

I devised a program to save money over the following few months. I added a large amount of Karen's check to our savings as well as my income from my pharmacy work and the occasional sale of a painting. I reduced or almost eliminated, temporarily, my spending on art materials. Each month, I paid a substantial amount off our credit card bill. It didn't take long until I paid off everything we owed.

I kept my part-time relief work for a while, even though it was far more stressful than working full-time when I knew my pharmacist partner and the people I worked with and was familiar with the layout of the pharmacy. As a roving pharmacist, they often called me to work at a one-man proprietor type of store in an outlying small town that I had never heard of. That meant I had no idea how the owner-pharmacist operated the pharmacy, always finding myself in a dire situation with a layout that had no rhyme or reason. It was an extremely unpredictable and stressful workload.

I got a phone call one day to work in a small store in a small town I had never known existed. It was out of sight, in a nook south on I-5. The day before I was scheduled to work, I went to the store to get the key to the pharmacy. The owner handed me the key, got in his car, and drove off. In the morning, I was at the store at eight thirty to open up and get myself acquainted with the pharmacy layout.

I unlocked the door and entered into a small, dimly lit store. I turned on the light and tried to explore the store setting, mostly the pharmacy and a few shelves with sundries. Only a few minutes had passed when suddenly a deafening alarm screamed. I had no inkling of the code or where to find the alarm box. There wasn't much to do except sweat it out. I waited, hoping I wouldn't get shot for breaking in. Soon a couple of police officers got out of their car with their hands by their belts in readiness.

Apprehensively, I walked out to meet them, identifying myself as a relief pharmacist. They located the alarm box and phoned the security company to silence it.

Soon the phone started ringing—first, a nurse phoning in a prescription. She was curt when I asked her to please repeat the name of the patient. The phone wouldn't stop ringing, and I was overwhelmed and flustered. Then it quieted down as swiftly as it had exploded. This was a small town with a small population. Customers were patient, aware of the situation I was in. A few said that it wasn't urgent that they get their prescription right away and would come back later in the afternoon.

Another time, I was scheduled to work for a couple of days in a small pharmacy in an Oregon coastal town. The pharmacy owner handed me the keys, told me he needed to leave right away, and showed me which key was for the store and which for his home. I would stay at his house while he was gone so he wouldn't worry about it being vacant.

After closing on a blustery evening, I drove on unfamiliar streets, looking for his house while the wind screamed, pine tops waved, and my VW bus shook. I could hardly identify houses, let alone house numbers.

When I finally found it, there wasn't much in the house, no furniture to speak of, and a lonely bed with no sheets or blankets. Not unlike what one might see in a prison cell. I took off my shoes and lay on the bed in my street clothes with the feeling that I was trespassing on someone else's privacy.

I may have dosed off for an hour when a roaring, water-fall-like sound startled me. I jumped out of bed frantic, disoriented, wondering where the heck I was. Was I in the midst of a dream? From the gabled roof that had no ceiling, what seemed like buckets of water poured down like a wide-open spigot, splashing on the wooden floor.

I had to do something. But what? I ran to the kitchen. Not much in there. *How did I get into this?* Opening a few cupboards, I found a pot. I ran to the bedroom and set it under the splashing water. It did little. With every drop, water sprang out of it as if in anger for the pot's presence, and splashed into a wider area of the floor. For what seemed an hour, I ran back and forth with the pot to the kitchen, spilling more water on my way. No use. It wasn't a puddle anymore.

Soon, the flow turned in to a drip, haunting me for what seemed like hours. I sat on the edge of the bed, socks soaked, shivering, gazing at the roof, watching water drops form. In agonizing, sporadic intervals, they dripped, dripped, dripped. I imagined their effectiveness in a sadistic torture environment. It was a sleepless night.

Nevertheless, I had much respect and appreciation for the local people in these small towns, despite the problems I sometimes faced. Their courtesy and patience were admirable. The busiest hours were usually the first few of the day, and, in most cases, for the rest of the day, I listened to customers' stories. The farmers and ranchers talked about horses, cattle, and sheep; teachers recommended their favorite books or movies; and store owners talked about how much they loved their town and for how long they had served the community.

CHAPTER 19

A Step into the Real

More and more, I gained confidence as a painter, and my art soon had an appeal that others noticed. Candy Moffett, a young woman with dark hair and dark eyes, who in a way reminded me of my sister Peggy, managed a small gallery at the corner of a room at Maude Kerns Art Center. She had seen my watercolor portrait paintings done at Maude Kerns and may have also seen a few of my landscapes and still lifes. She offered to show a few of my small-format watercolor sketches that she liked.

At some point, Candy opened her own gallery on Alder Street in Eugene and named it Alder Gallery. She asked me for several large oil figurative, still life, and landscape paintings. I became one of her prominent artists. She loved and promoted my work. And through her energy, sales of my work grew. Sales weren't limited to landscape and still life but also included the figurative, and were not limited to one medium. She carried my paintings in oil, watercolor, and pastel.

Through Candy's effort, the California Bank in Eugene commissioned me to do large paintings of Oregon scenes. In the past, I had shied away from taking commissions, yet in this case I couldn't say no. I did a couple of very large landscape paintings in acrylics. They liked them and had them in a permanent installation on a wall of the bank in prominent view. And they paid me more than I expected.

Candy also gave me a one-person show at the Hilton Hotel in Eugene. The Hilton had an enormous lobby, and when I saw my large paintings displayed on its walls, I was able to see my artwork through the eyes of others. It was an impressive exhibit.

Then Candy moved her gallery to nearby Coburg, a lovely small town. And there again, I was one of her top artists in sales. In her gallery, I met wonderful artists, among them Jill Atkin and Philip Roberts. Phil had his own style, a high-key impressionist style that Karen and I liked. We became good friends and painted outdoors together for quite a while until he moved to Portland.

Eventually, Candy bought one of my still-life paintings herself, and I was proud and delighted that she had that confidence in my work. She often took estate paintings to sell at her gallery and kept them in her back room. She phoned me one day to tell me she had one of Bongart's paintings for $800. Without seeing it, I told her I wanted it. It ended up being a twenty-by-twenty-four-inch painting of a night scene, somber with deep dark blues and blacks all over, with a few figures and streetlights in red and orange, painted with a palette knife, a style unusual for Bongart. I loved it, and so did Karen. I'm proud that I own one of his paintings. It hangs on our wall.

Unfortunately, Candy had to close her gallery when she was diagnosed with a brain tumor. She went through chemo and radiation therapy. I was doing a demo one evening at Maude Kerns when a friend of Candy's brought her along. On one hand, I was delighted to see her, but it also saddened me. I almost didn't recognize her at that stage of her illness.

She was happy to see me. Soon after, she passed on.

She had been the one who believed in me as an artist and promoted me. Because of her energy and enthusiasm for my work, I became a well-known artist in this area. With her passing, I lost a friend and an influential supporter.

Gallery Chevrielle, in Yachats, on the Oregon coast north of Florence, was another venue that showed and sold my artwork. Charlotte and her photographer husband ran the gallery of contemporary artists. They both had an interest in my work. They promoted and sold quite a few of my paintings in the coastal towns. I admired their gallery artists, including Vernon Nye, a superb old school California watercolorist. He was a humble man who once told me the reason he was a member of the prestigious American Watercolor Society, which required a high standard of proficiency to be accepted as a member, was because of when he applied. He said his work wouldn't match the work of the contemporary experimental watercolor artist members of today.

The Chevrielle gallery closed in Yachats, but they opened a gallery by the same name in Calistoga, California, where they also represented my artwork. Not long after, Charlotte also contracted cancer. They closed the gallery and shipped back my paintings. Not too long after that, she passed on.

Once, when I was in the right place and at the right time, someone happened to take a photo of me painting plein air. It was early morning, and I was at Mount Pisgah Arboretum, a beautiful park I had painted in a few times. I set up my easel by the side of a dirt road. Shadows of trees and bushes crossed the road. Intermittent bands of light streaked through them. I was in the middle of the painting when someone with a camera came by and asked if it was okay to take photos of me painting. "Of course," I said. He took photos and handed me a card that I placed in my shirt pocket and thought little about. The next morning, I was painting at the same park in a different location. Several women came by to show me the *Register-Guard* newspaper. On the front page was a photo of me painting the day before.

A longtime artist in Eugene emailed me: "I have never seen a photo of any artist on the front page of the newspaper until now." In the past, they had photos of artists and their artwork in the art section of the newspaper, but never on the front page.

Over the following years, newspapers in Eugene and in other towns in Oregon featured me in various articles. In 1984, *The Junction City Times* featured me in an article titled "Onetime pharmacist seeks a new image." It showed two of my watercolor paintings.

In 1986, the Sunriver Art Fair competition selected my watercolor painting *Oregon Coast*. The jurors were Donald Jenkins, director of the Portland Art Museum, and Eve Slinker, president and founder of the Eastern Oregon Regional Arts Council and member of the Oregon Arts Commission. I was featured in an article by Sally Schoolmaster, titled "Seeks life in his paintings."

Also in 1986, the Portland Art Museum Rental Sales Gallery featured me in an exhibition article titled "News from Maude's."

In 1987, the Pastel Society of America selected my painting in a juried show in New York exhibited in the gallery of the National Arts Club.

In 1991, a color image of my oil painting *Sailboats* was on the cover of the magazine *48° North*, the sailing magazine.

In June 1991, a color image of one of my still lifes was on the cover of the Oregon Public Broadcasting magazine.

In 1998, I was featured in the *Register-Guard*'s art and entertainment section along with my full-page photo on the section's front page.

Two of my watercolor paintings are on poet Frannie Lindsay's poetry book covers: My watercolor painting *Lamb* was on her book titled *Lamb*, published in 2006, and my watercolor painting *Tenderly* was on her book titled *If Mercy*, published in 2016.

One day, out of the blue, I received a phone call from Joseph, my ex-brother-in-law. He said he had followed my artistic career and loved my paintings. He asked if I would create an oil painting of one of his landscape photographs. Joseph had been instrumental in initiating my artistic journey the day I watched him paint a still life in oils at our home. I was then in my teens, and until that day, I had never seen any other living painter. Joseph's passion for the arts either hadn't lasted or remained limited in its scope. He didn't pursue painting with the passion and determination to succeed as an artist.

I accepted the challenge with the stipulation that I would keep the painting if he had any reservations about the outcome. He mailed me the photo, a landscape of trees with a rowboat moored in a lake in the lower left corner. He asked if I would paint the word *Ramian*, his last name, on the side of the boat since the painting was meant to be a legacy for his daughters.

The photo was old and faded with blurred shapes. I took liberties in color and interpretation, and I named the boat *Ramian* as he requested. He liked the results but couldn't refrain from noting the liberties that I had taken. Nevertheless, he sent me a check.

More and more, I came to believe that many, especially other artists, considered me a renowned painter. For quite a few years, others couldn't accept that a pharmacist could turn into an artist overnight. They assumed art was a hobby I dabbled in. Eventually, seeing my work in galleries and articles written about me in newspapers, the public accepted me as an artist. As time passed, some learned of my previous pharmacy career. It might have been a surprise, yet to them it had no relevance.

CHAPTER 20

A Path to Contentment

Even though I kept my pharmacy relief work, we were falling back into debt. Then, out of the blue, I received a call from Dave Thompson, a pharmacist I had worked with in the past. He said, "Sarkis, I need your help." He was the pharmacy manager at Tiffany's Drugstore at the Oakway mall in Eugene. His call caught me by surprise.

"When?" I asked.

"Right away. Now," he said. It would be full-time work. He had a temporary pharmacist, but he needed someone permanently.

I told Karen I was about to take a full-time job. "Why would you want to do that?" she asked.

"Our finances are pretty bad. I have to do something."

When I arrived at the pharmacy, patients were waiting, and Dave and the other pharmacist were dealing with a chaotic situation, answering nonstop phone calls and filling prescriptions for anxious patients.

"Good to see you. We need you here," Dave said.

In that hectic environment, I felt lost, as I had been out of my pharmacy career since I quit PayLess and had focused on painting ever since. I stood there helpless. I didn't have time to look around and figure out their setup to even do the clerk's work of at least retrieving drugs or having the courage to answer the phones while Dave and his other pharmacist were frantically trying to keep up with the incoming prescriptions.

Disheartened, I concluded that my presence would only hinder the operation of the pharmacy. At the end of the day, I told Dave, "This will not work for me. I can't handle it."

He looked at me. "Don't worry," he said, "Sunday, we'll work together. It's never a busy day, and we'll work it out. I need you here."

I wondered if escaping my insecurities would ever be possible.

I worked with Dave for five years, only the two of us. We worked in harmony. During this time, Dale and Melva Engel moved from the East Coast to Oregon, bought the drugstore from Mrs. Tiffany, and became the owners of Tiffany's Drugstore.

When, around 1989, Dale closed the Oakway mall store, I transferred to the Tiffany's Drugstore in a small shopping center in Veneta, ten miles south of our home. Here, I worked with Joel, the pharmacy manager, until 1994, the year that was a critical turning point in my life. I was sixty-two years old and would be an early Social Security recipient. I had been working at the drugstore in Veneta for five years and intended to inform management that my career as a practicing pharmacist was at an end.

The night before I was going to give my notice, I stayed late, revisiting how my career in pharmacy had begun—an impulsive choice about something I knew nothing about and had no interest in. With shallow reasoning I had believed it would only be of a short duration. Yet it continued, on and on, for thirty-five restless years.

By this time, with habitual saving and judicious investing, Karen and I found ourselves in a comfortable financial position. Of particular importance for me was the fact that my steep art expenses weren't a major burden anymore, diminishing the guilt that weighed on me.

Now with my pharmacy career behind me, most people would have thought that taking on a new demanding and complex career late in life would seem irrational. But for me, a new and exciting chapter in my life was starting. I looked at the world in a different light. Not unlike when I was in my teens, I still envisioned a sublime way of life in art. Even though I had a clear understanding that the art of painting would be a never-ending learning process, I delved into it with abandon.

I dismissed the unsettling thoughts and memories of the years when I was apologetic about dabbling in the craft of painting. Now I didn't shy away from saying "I am a painter," but I still couldn't bring myself to say, "I am an artist."

My approach to painting was fast and intuitive, oblivious to any methodical working habit or style. I became an experimental painter in most known genres—figurative, landscape, and still life. In time, my successes outnumbered my failures. My inventory of work expanded, and I soon ran out of storage space. In 1997, I decided to build an addition to my studio. Karen suggested we hire a contractor to add a two-story, spacious addition to the one I had built. The lower space would be a gallery to display my paintings for interested buyers, since by this time I had begun to sell my artwork.

The top level of the addition became my workplace

whenever I wasn't painting outdoors, but more so it was my retreat—a space with a ten-foot picture window overlooking our walnut orchard and our two barns. Through this window, an unobstructed view far beyond our land extends for miles— ryegrass fields stretching all the way to blue-green hills of fir trees on the horizon, a spectacular scene under a magnificent sky—a scene I have painted over and over, in all seasons and climate conditions. Here, in my retreat, I have my art books, my art supplies, my short stories, and my music. In this environment, I am in a state of happiness and contentment being the person who I always yearned to be.

PART IV

TRAVEL AND REFLECTIONS

CHAPTER 21

Oregon—How I See It

It's been years since we moved to Oregon. My initial impression of our lovely state hasn't changed. I still see its landscape through the eyes of a tourist awed by its picture-perfect beauty. Throughout its four distinct seasons, its hues pulsate as if scanning a rainbow, one minute to the next radiating creative energy—a haven for an aspiring artist.

Weather in the Willamette Valley is temperate. In winter we get some rain, a mild freeze, or occasional snowfall that in most years exquisitely blankets the landscape for only a few days. We may have a few hundred-degree days in summer. Yet none of the fluctuations in weather throughout the seasons have been extreme, prolonged, or intolerable. And none have ever dampened my affection for my adopted state.

Spring in Oregon is especially spectacular. Meadows can be yellow greens, deep greens, or grass greens. Buds on fruit trees swell early in February and by early March erupt into white or pink blossoms tinged with the sky's cobalt blue. White, yellow, or purple crocuses show their faces in January. Tulips and daffodils blossom in gardens and along roads and highways year after year.

Mild winters with dry summers in the Willamette Valley make it ideal to produce high-quality rye seed. Around June and July, soon after farmers thresh and bale the straw, you can see bleached-ochre ryegrass fields everywhere. On overcast days, the fields turn vivid red or mahogany. In summer, the light green-and-red maple leaves complement the dense deep green of the majestic firs. Autumn is another season of color: gold and orange.

Glorious pink rhododendrons are native to Oregon, and they are all over the hills and pastures of the coastal range. A variety of pink, lavender, or mottled white rhododendrons, and red, salmon, and lavender azaleas appear in many yards and parks in Lane County. Aside from the native coastal rhododendrons, native wildflowers in parks also attest to Oregon's natural beauty. All over Oregon, luscious rose blossoms—red, magenta, pink, yellow, orange, and lavender—appear throughout summer and fall months in gardens and parks. Portland is known as the "City of Roses." Portland's International Rose Test Garden is in an impressive setting among evergreens. It overlooks part of downtown Portland and Mount Hood and is a spectacular attraction for thousands of visitors from all over the world as well as the many Portlanders who never tire of enjoying the sight and scent of their own rose garden.

In Eugene, my favorite hangout spots are Hendricks Park, Owen Rose Garden, and Mount Pisgah Arboretum, where I have spent many hours painting.

Hendricks Park is the oldest city park. Its eighty acres include the world-renowned rhododendron garden. Native plants, wildflowers, and varieties of ground cover skirt trails that are a retreat for hikers and nature lovers.

Hendricks Park was only a mile from Tiffany's Drugstore. On my lunch hour, I would drive to the park and eat my bag lunch, sitting on a bench in a serene setting among rhododendrons and azaleas, far from the hectic and stressful pharmacy environment.

Owen Rose Garden is an eight-and-a-half-acre Willamette riverfront park. Besides its impressive heritage and heirloom rose garden, it features an immense Oregon heritage cherry tree, benches, a pergola covered with vines over paved walkways, and an immense twenty-eight-foot gazebo and picnic area. When I worked at Valu-Mart drugstore on Second Street in downtown Eugene, I spent my lunch hour at Owen Rose Garden, within walking distance from the store.

Another notable park that I often visit, a painter's retreat, is the Mount Pisgah Arboretum. It's a 209-acre nature preserve southeast of downtown Eugene. Its trails wind along the river through a variety of trees and wildflowers. It's a place to explore nature in its display of wildflowers and wildlife. In May, the park features a yearly wildflower and music festival. In October they sponsor a mushroom festival.

The Oregon coast has always been inspiring with subjects that I returned to over and over in my artistic career. Years ago, on Fridays at the end of my day shift at the pharmacy, I'd get in my VW van and head to Newport on a weekend painting trip. I always slept in the van to save money. We bought the van used. It had wild designs that made little sense. People who by chance saw it parked in a parking lot assumed the owner was a shaggy-looking hippie. In the back of the van I had my sleeping bag and a pillow. My mind wasn't on comfort, it was on the next day's painting excursion, with almost a feverish expectation—where would I set my easel, what would I be looking at, and how would I paint it.

I'd leave before daybreak and drive to my favorite harbor in Newport. It would take me around two hours to arrive on the outskirts of Newport. I'd find a vacant lot and park, hoping that no one would show up and tell me to move on. There used to be a perfect accessible area at the harbor, overlooking a variety of subjects to paint. I would paint the anchored boats, the arched bridge, and the view of the shoreline around the harbor. As many times as I have sketched and painted the scene from this location, it was never the same. There always was a newness that provoked excitement.

Another favorite harbor of mine is in Depoe Bay. One day, I set my easel on the walkway overlooking the anchored boats, the bridge, and a few homes on the hill, and while I was halfway into my painting, a man in a dress shirt, tie, and sport coat walked by. He said he liked what was on my canvas and that he was associated with the city's Chamber of Commerce, and that seeing artists at work in parks and harbors was good for tourism.

Soon after the man left, a gust of wind blew my wooden palette over. It hit the cement sidewalk paint-side down. When I picked up the palette, I saw thick globs of oil paint covering a square-foot area of the sidewalk. I tried to wipe the paint off, using almost half of my roll of paper towels. But the more I rubbed, the wider the spot spread. Luckily, no one was around. I quickly packed my easel, palette, and half-finished painting and left the harbor. Next day, after painting all day at a different location, I drove to the Depoe Bay harbor. Without my painting gear, incognito, I found the spot of my mishap had no trace of color—almost a miracle. Relieved, I decided to explore other painting locations and found an out-of-the-way, tranquil grassy area where I could set up and paint the boats, the bridge, and the homes on the hill.

Over the years, I made several coastal-painting weekends, focusing on different locations on the coast. Florence and Yachats have always been my favorite painting towns closest to home. Florence is only an hour's drive away. It has a beautiful harbor, large parking area, and a walkway by the harbor that is a perfect place to set up my easel to paint the tugboats and the shoreline of green hills. I often included Mo's restaurant. Sometimes I'd walk down the ramp by the restaurant and paint, standing on the dock platform—a spot that has a fabulous view of the bridge and the colorful buildings high on a steep hill by the shore.

Yachats is a half hour north of Florence on Highway 101. Right before entering Yachats, I would pull over onto a short semi-circular driveway that connected with the highway at the other end. It is a park-like exit that has benches and a great view. I would set up my easel at a spot overlooking the town high above a cove—a magnificent view of colorful homes, shops, and restaurants along Highway 101, backed by fir-covered hills.

In Yachats, another favorite of my subjects is the rocky beach at Smelt Sands State Park. It's a popular smelt fishing beach between April and October. It is said that Yachats is one of the few beaches in Oregon where the smelt, a sardine-like fish, come to the shore to spawn. This is the time when many from other states visit Yachats to fish and can net mounds of smelt easily.

I also enjoyed painting at Winchester Bay, a half hour drive south of Florence. I loved to paint the fishing boats and the colorful buildings by the harbor.

When my brother visited us, I took him salmon fishing on a charter boat at Winchester Bay Salmon Harbor. I was pleased that we each caught one fish. It was an exciting fishing excursion and made his Oregon visit even more memorable.

In July 2017, Karen and I decided to take a three-week trip to explore the coastal towns and beaches of Oregon. We asked Garrick, our daughter-in-law Bethany, and grandkids to stay at our place while we were gone. At the time, Garrick worked from home and was able to do this.

I took small boards and gouache paint so I could sketch whenever I had the chance. When we were out of the wind in the comfort of our motel room, I'd paint from photos and memory what I had seen and experienced during the day.

Our trip began in Astoria, a coastal town in the northwest corner of Oregon that we had visited many years before. From that trip, we recalled the *Peter Iredale* shipwreck at Fort Stevens State Park, a few miles south of Astoria. The ship sank a hundred years ago on its way to Portland. During our first trip, I painted a large oil painting of it, accentuating its skeletal rust colors—shades of deep red, green, and yellow. What astonished us during this trip was how much it had sunk since then—a few parts of it have completely disappeared.

During this trip our intent was to visit the many Oregon towns and harbors along Highway 101 that Karen and I hadn't visited in the past, towns and beaches such as the one in Oswald West State Park, a secluded sandy beach sheltered in a cove protected from wind by forests, basalt, and sandstone cliffs, that made strolling on its windless, sandy beach a joy; lovely Manzanita beach; and Garibaldi Marina that is an especially beautiful subject for an artist with its tugboats moored against a lovely stretch of blue-green hills. When we passed Siletz Bay, I remembered the day on one of my solo trips when I had parked and set my easel by the highway, painting the rocks below—at a safe place to park while cars and trucks barreled by me. From my position, beside the rocks, there was a fantastic view of a stretch of some of Lincoln City's shoreline buildings.

At Coos Bay near Charleston, an artist friend suggested that I go to a dry dock that had a lot of painting subjects. It had boats large and small hoisted up for maintenance. I painted a few gouache paintings of the boats. From a photo I had taken, I did a YouTube video painting demo of one of the boats at the site.

Port Orford was interesting in that the parking lot was high above the ocean. A string of boats was on the edge of the parking lot, backed by a tall, dark, rocky outcrop. This was the subject of one of my two small gouache paintings. When we walked down to the sandy beach, looking up at the same parking lot to get a different view, there was a beautiful blue dry-docked boat. Next to it was a stack of yellow and orange canoes by a small white shack. This was the subject of my second painting. Of the first small painting, I did a large demo at the University of Oregon Duck Store during their yearly trade shows.

What is especially valuable about Oregon beaches is that

they are open to the public at all times. There are no private beaches. Driving on Highway 101, Oregon's coastal route, was a pleasurable exploration of our beautiful Oregon coastal towns and beaches. It also gave me plenty of subjects for large oil and acrylic pictures done either from the small gouache paintings or the many photos we took.

The impression I get listening to those who have never lived in Oregon throughout the seasons is they believe that in this state, and especially in the Willamette Valley, it rains a lot. They may have a view of it as being wet and gloomy. We own raincoats and rubber boots, but I don't recall ever wearing them more than a couple of times, if any, during the year.

Although rain depresses some people, for me, raindrops are enlivening and energizing. On a rainy day, the landscape has a beauty of its own. On a wintry day, when I look out my studio's picture window, golden ryegrass blankets the ground around our walnut trees, whose trunks are black silhouettes, their branches like fingers pointing at the sky. Often crows adorn the branches like black gemstones. Water droplets snake down my picture window in rivulets.

When it's raining, I have the urge to do something just for my pleasure or comfort. In an uncluttered state of tranquility, on a rainy day, I paint, write, or even daydream.

CHAPTER 22

The Middle East

In 1998, my sisters Aleece and Alexandra suggested the four of us travel to Beirut and Amman for a family reunion. Instead of a jubilant response, I succumbed to the regrets that had haunted me for years. I questioned all the excuses I had created in my mind not to go back home to visit my family when my parents were alive and was burdened by my mother's persistent request to send a postcard to say I was doing well, which I had failed to do. Now, my sisters cautioned me not to make the same mistake and to take this opportunity to be with the rest of my family at a reunion. Most of my family, except for my nephew Serop and his wife, Talene, had met Karen in the US. Visiting Jordan, the country where I was born and had lived for twenty-five years of my life, would be an especially exciting trip for Karen, who had just retired. She would have a chance to stay in the house where I grew up and often talked about and described in detail. She would even sleep in the same room I slept in until I left for the US in 1958. It would also be the first time in thirty-five years that all five of us siblings would be together.

I had told Karen a few stories about my first home in the vicinity of the Roman amphitheater in Amman. That's the home where I was born and lived until I was around five or six years old. During those years, in my recollection, an unpaved road passed by the house, and once a month, on a wide dusty area across from our house, exciting things happened. Bedouins left their wives and small children in black or brown woolen tents erected a few kilometers from the city and, with their teenage boys, converged on this dusty area to sell or to barter their livestock for city goods. My sisters Peggy and Alexandra and I were allowed to go out and watch this thrilling activity. The men and the boys mingled with their livestock as if they were family. They were armed with sticks. With a gesture, a gentle tap, and a whisper, the Bedouins managed to have the whole spectacle under control. Although the area had no boundaries to contain the livestock, no sheep broke away, no goat strayed, no camel broke loose. There was a day when a camel seemed to be mad for a little while. It frothed at the mouth, uttering frightening sounds. With a gentle maneuver of his stick, a Bedouin moved the animal around in a circle until it knelt down and settled by its master, content and calm, its huge dangling lips in perpetual chewing motion, oblivious to its surroundings.

My mother had created work for needy Arab women and girls. A few of them lived at our house. Those who went home to their own families at the end of the day were given leftover food and sometimes clothing. My mother had even hired Sabha, a woman who may have had syphilis or leprosy, who had lost her nose and had sores around the cavity in the middle of her face. She covered her head and face, except for her jet-black eyes, with a black cloth. When I was six or seven years old, I sometimes sat next to her and watched her grind wheat with our millstone. She would turn the top stone round and round, grinding the wheat. Her veil would often slip off, exposing the sores on her face. She would quickly pick up the veil and cover her face again. She must have appreciated my keeping her company, as one day she brought me a cute, fluffy black chick. My pet chick turned into a noisy rooster.

My father often said to my mother that she should be careful about exposing us young children to sick people like Sabha. She would tell him not to worry. "God will protect them."

I had told Karen of the yearly festivities that were held in the arena of the amphitheater, during which Peggy, Alexandra, and I spent a couple of days with Im-Saeed. She was one of the women my mother hired to do odd jobs.

Im-Saeed, with her sixteen-year-old son, Saeed, and her ten-year-old daughter, Hawwa, lived in a cave-like home close to where we lived. Her home had a dirt floor that was packed solid through constant treading to make a solid surface to walk or sleep on. It was the room where she also cooked their meals. Next to it was a small room where Saeed made ice pops that he sold at the amphitheater during the yearly festival. Whatever process he used to create them is still a mystery to me. I remember him dumping crystals on ice blocks in a couple of barrels around the molds that shaped the popsicles. It took a few days to get those ice pops hard enough to transport to the arena of the amphitheater. We helped him carry stuff and were rewarded by sampling one of the glistening blue, red, and yellow ice pops before we got to the arena.

Im-Saeed fed us *fattoush*, a salad that we loved. It was a mix of dry bread, tomatoes, parsley, green onions, and a succulent slimy plant called *baaleh*, that looked like purslane but with larger edible leaves—a tasteless vegetable that added green to the meal. She took us to a nearby field to pick the baaleh. We picked some, but mostly played while she did most of the picking. Back at her home, she placed all the needed ingredients outside on a table by a faucet. She washed greens and tomatoes, then chopped them on a wooden board that was darkened by use. In a bowl, she combined all the vegetables, added the dry bread, lemon juice, olive oil, pepper, and salt, and tossed it all together to make a meal that I miss to this day.

Early in the morning, with festive spirit, we accompanied Saeed with his popsicles to the arena of the amphitheater, where other young men sold falafel, hummus, peanuts, pumpkin seeds, and *kdameh* (garbanzo nuts).

In the arena, there were a couple of bulky swings large enough to seat two or three children. They were heavy and only gave a hint of motion. Even then, we waited eagerly for our turns.

For young adult males, there were a couple of swings that had skateboard-size platforms attached to ropes, tied to over fifteen-feet-high scaffolding. Awed, I watched the fearless young men standing on the small platforms, and with a few contortions of body and legs, swinging in rhythm, one minute crouching and the next minute straight-up, flying higher and higher, building momentum, until like birds they seemed to reach the sky.

We climbed the massive steps of the theater with hardly a notion that Romans had sat on these very steps, watching the entertainment of the time. Men fought men and men fought beasts, not for any legitimate reason but for the pleasure of the civilized people who cheered or booed, thumbs up or thumbs down, while participants tore at each other and blood spilled. We investigated the rooms that were on top of the steps that may have been where the emperor and his entourage sat as they were entertained with a full view of the arena.

At the time of our visit, the environment surrounding the amphitheater had transformed unimaginably. Across from where our house used to be, there was a wide paved road. I hardly recognized the arena. It had stores and eateries—a touristy environment.

I was delighted to find that our house on Jabal Amman, where we moved when I was six years old and stayed until I left for the US, was almost the same. The garden on the top level around our house and the veranda were even more beautiful and exotic. The lower area had been remodeled into a beautiful dwelling for Serop and Talene. Vivid blue trim adorned the outdoor windows and doors, and there were hanging baskets. Serop's apartment replaced the old lower rooms of our house, including the room where we had our oven. The washroom I used to sneak into for a smoke had become a storage room. The adobe chicken coop of my childhood had been torn down and rebuilt into another storage room. The ground where we had our vegetable garden and where I raised rabbits had also changed. The apricot trees that I used to climb on and from which I cut forked branches to make slingshots were gone.

Amman had changed dramatically from when I left in 1958. Its population then was around 250,000. At the time of our visit, its population was over two million.

Serop took us to the Citadel and its museum. Among the prominent people who had inhabited Amman were the Ammonites in the thirteenth century BC. They made it flourish as their capital and named it Rabat Ammon. At the Citadel, at the edge of the city, remnants of that capital still exist.

We walked to the CMS, the Christian Missionary School, which Peggy and Alexandra and I attended. Beyond third grade, it was a girls-only school. And that's when I continued my schooling in Jerusalem. It was a short walk from our home. Often in the morning, walking to school, my sisters and I held bouquets of flowers from our garden that my mother created for us to take to our teachers.

Hussein, who eventually became the king of Jordan, lived with his father, Emir Talal, in a house close to our home. He had also attended CMS. He may have been in first grade when I was in third. Hussein gifted me with my first bicycle, a two-wheeler with solid tires.

We took a taxi to my high school, Terra Sancta. Entering the classrooms with the wide windows along a corridor reminded me of Brother Anthony, the principal, a heavy-set, tough man who walked past the windows, up and down the corridor, hands clasped behind his back. His appearance intimidated us students and unnerved the teachers, who were distracted every few minutes by his overpowering presence.

The tan desks seemed pretty much the same, with scratches and ink stains, not unlike the desk that I'd had. I was tempted to see if my initials were engraved under the lid of one of the desks.

We took a few memorable trips around Jordan, including

to Ma'in's therapeutic hot spring. Its pool and waterfall had a temperature of ninety degrees. It took us a few minutes to acclimate to the hot temperature. We swam in the Red Sea in Aqaba and had a swim, or rather a bob, in the Dead Sea where we also smeared the black mud, presumed to be therapeutic, over our bodies from neck to toes.

In Amman, one evening, we dined at Kan Zamaan, which means "It was a long time ago." The restaurant had a unique Bedouin ambience with waiters dressed in Bedouin garb. There were rooms where artisans blew glass in fascinating colors and shapes, and other artisans filled bottles with multicolor layers of sand. There was music, singing, dancing, and delicious food.

Our explorations took us to many archaeological wonders in that part of the world. We traveled to Jerash, which is considered one of the largest and most well-preserved sites of Roman architecture in the world outside of Italy. We visited Petra, the historic and archaeological city with its palaces, temples, tombs, and stables carved into vivid red, white, and pink sandstone cliffs. To get to the narrow passages of the picturesque and breathtaking cliffs, we had to walk or ride a camel a long distance over sandy ground. Karen had the opportunity to ride a camel while Alexandra and I walked with a boy and two Bedouin girls. Both girls had jet-black eyes and black hair and strands of hair peeked out of the dusty gray headdress of one of the girls. They gave Alexandra and Karen bracelets they had made.

We flew to Beirut to visit Peggy, who had returned home. In the 1950s, the view of the Mediterranean Sea from their veranda, at night or daytime, was spectacular. Now their home was surrounded by two or three-story houses blocking any view beyond a few yards. But her garden was still exotic, with a variety of fruit trees and tropical flowers. I did a few paintings of her garden.

My niece Helena and her husband, Nadeem, took us to their condo in Brummana, where we stayed overnight and marveled at the spectacular view of the Mediterranean. We were extremely thankful to Helena. We couldn't have asked for a better guide during the days we spent in Lebanon. She took us to the AUB that I wanted so badly to visit, and we walked through the campus as I had done many years ago as a student. Even though it didn't look familiar at first, as we walked through the campus, I couldn't help but get the feeling that, yes, I was here before.

I picked a carob bean from a tree and took a bite, as I had done when I was around eighteen or nineteen years old attending the university. It also reminded me of when I lived in the Old City of Jerusalem with Aleece, and I rode my bicycle to Terra Sancta school in the new city. On the way, I would stop to pick a few carob beans off trees that were near the sidewalks.

We walked down the hill to the campus' rocky beach. Helena got permission for us to swim there even though it's a private beach for students and faculty. It was especially exciting because that was where I had learned how to swim.

Helena drove us to Bsharri, the hometown of Khalil Gibran. Along the highway, the views were breathtaking: scenic hills and mountains peppered by pines and white houses with red-orange brick roofs. I have always believed that Lebanon is one of the most beautiful countries in the world.

On our way to Bsharri, we came upon a herd of black goats crossing the road. They seemed unperturbed by our presence. We stopped and waited. It was quite a sight. We hadn't yet seen any other car or human, and here was a Bedouin with his goats, all taking their time crossing the road. When I attended the university in Beirut, a couple of schoolmates and I hiked on some of these hills. Often, we came upon villages where the villagers offered us fruit and sparkling water to whet our thirst. Once, when we were thirsty and tired of climbing steep hills, we came upon a shallow mountain stream with what seemed to be crystal clear water. We got down on our knees to have a drink of the cool water. A goat herder showed up out of nowhere with his goats and told us to stop what we were about to do. He wanted to show us what was in the water. He pooled some in his palms and there they were: tiny pink leeches. We could hardly see them. Swallowing a leech that would hang on somewhere inside our throats, suck blood, and grow to choke us was a horrible thought.

Bsharri is a lovely village with markets and vendors all around its streets. Khalil Gibran's home is on a hillside. It housed a gallery of his paintings, mostly dark and poetic. His book, *The Prophet*, has never been out of print. It's among the top ten most translated books in history and was one of the best-selling books of the twentieth century in the United States.

Gibran has always been one of my favorite poets, writers, and painters. I've never tired of picking up one of his books at random to read a paragraph or two for my own enjoyment, if not for my enlightenment.

His dark and depressing paintings are in the Brooklyn Museum and the Metropolitan Museum of Art. They portray the complexity of the artist.

Back in Amman, we walked down the steep road toward the city center to visit my brother's music shop, passing the house where Emir Talal and his son Hussein used to live.

In our teens, my cousin Haig and I discovered a steep rocky hill off this paved road, which seemed to us a shortcut to the city center. I remembered the day Haig and I were going down this rocky shortcut hill; I was slipping and sliding, trying to catch up with him, when I fell. A piece of glass cut a long, deep gash on my kneecap. I almost fainted upon seeing blood spurting from my leg. Haig took off his shirt and wrapped it around my knee and just about carried me down the hill. I still have the scar as a testament to that day. During our visit, I noticed the hill hadn't changed at all and was still a rocky, barren incline.

Downtown, we walked among throngs of Arab men and women taking in the ambience of the old town shopping area, a narrow tunnel-like enclosed path with shops on both sides. This hadn't changed at all—presenting a dazzling array of enticing merchandise, loaded with a variety of odds and ends, jewelry, brightly colored dresses and scarves, artifacts, pots, and pans. It was fun to discover the unusual. There, when I was a boy, I bought caps for my cap gun, and my brother bought ammunition for rifle target practice.

We took a bus to Jerusalem. The Allenby Bridge on the

Jordan River separates Israel from Jordan. The bridge crosses a trickle of water—not much of a river now, whereas in the old days, when all the area was Jordanian land, the river was wide and deep. During those years, many religious people claimed that the fish in the Jordan River had the sign of a cross on their heads.

In Jerusalem, we stayed at a hotel at Notre Dame of Jerusalem Center across from the Old City. Standing by the gate to the Old City reminded me of the years when I lived with Aleece and Vahan. After spending weekends in Amman, on Sundays, I would travel to Jerusalem in a taxi with adult passengers. The taxi would drop us off a few yards from the gate to the Old City. This was a terrifying time for me. I would immediately be surrounded by a group of tough, barefoot boys my age or even much younger. Many hands would pull the small handbag I carried and struggled to keep a hold on. I would soon lose my grip and a triumphant kid with a big smile on his face would walk away with it. But not too far. His intention was to carry my bag for a few piasters. As the driver set my heavy suitcase on the ground, immediately a large man with a thick rope and a leather strap swung on his shoulder would pick it up.

Vahan, expecting my arrival, would save me from this out-of-control situation. He would give the boy who had my handbag a few piasters and would immediately negotiate a fee with the man who already had my luggage strapped to his back. There we were, the three of us, Vahan, the man, and I, walking past the Old City gate, fighting our way through the crowd of mostly Arabs and the few tourists who purchased religious artifacts from shops that lined these alleys. I often fell a few steps behind, fighting the throng of people all around me in that crowded, cobbled alley, almost running to stay close to Vahan and the man. A few donkeys packed with heavy loads would push their way through the crowd. I was always alerted that they were right behind me by the clicking sound of their hooves on the cobbled stones.

Now, as an adult entering the Armenian Quarter, my interest focused on Aleece's apartment on the top level across from the Agoump, the Armenian Club. Standing on the cobblestone alley, I looked up at the window of the room where, when I was a young boy, I slept, did my schoolwork, and drew. The adjacent club wasn't the same as I remembered it. It seemed almost deserted. During my stay at my sister's home, the club was the center of Armenian activity. They had dances, sports activities, and the scout program—all young Armenian men were boy scouts and all boys, including me, were cub scouts.

On our way back to Amman, we drove through Jericho. I have a pleasant memory of Jericho and the orange orchards that were everywhere. When I was a medical representative on my route to Jerusalem, the taxi driver often stopped in Jericho. We'd have a cup of coffee at a coffee shop surrounded by orange orchards. I would almost be in a trance, imagining myself living in an imaginary home surrounded by such fruit trees.

In Amman, Karen and I slept in my old room (and maybe even my own bed) from when I was six years old until I flew to the US. I sat next to my brother, Ohanness, under the grape arbor by the side of the house while he grilled shish kabob. He had an electric fan to keep the coals red hot. It was a pleasant time for the two of us having a beer and sampling the shish kabob wrapped in pieces of flat bread. Hnaz, my lovely sister-in-law, did her best to accommodate us, cooking all day long—not only the meals she usually prepared but also the vegetarian meals she cooked, especially for Karen and me, which everyone else sampled and enjoyed. My sisters and I are thankful for Hnaz. She took care not only of her aged parents but also my mother and father while my sisters and I lived abroad. It wasn't long after we got back from our Middle East Trip that Hnaz was diagnosed with a brain tumor and was in a coma for a while, then passed on, and so did Ohanness soon after. Seeing them before they left us relieved me of some of the guilt and regrets I had harbored for years, due to not seeing my parents before they passed on, as I had promised. This had weighed on me for so long.

Of our Middle Eastern trip, I painted over sixty watercolor paintings of Lebanon, Jordan, and Israel.

CHAPTER 23

Painting Trips and Workshops

Charles Sovek is an artist I have admired for years, so when I saw he was giving a workshop in April 2003 in Scottsdale, Arizona, I had the urge to visit the town that I had heard so much about and participate in this amazing artist's workshop.

He was the contributing editor to *Artist* magazine for twenty years, and through his extensive writing, he gained a worldwide reputation. His early work was detailed no differently from any other artist of the time. Over the years, he adopted a smaller format in his paintings and a much simpler expressionistic style that I admired and desired to emulate or incorporate in my work.

In his demos, with a simple palette of the three primaries plus black and white, he captured the essence of the subject in a few vivid colors and simplified shapes. I was inspired and energized, adopting the philosophy that art need not be complicated to be effective.

In 2004, I decided to participate in another of Sovek's workshops, this time in Cape Cod. What I remember of this workshop is his ten-by-eight-inch painting of a woman sitting outdoors on a chair. In his demo, he portrayed her character as well as an undeniable likeness with as little detail as possible. I am proud to own this small painting.

In Provincetown, I painted a few scenes of the harbor as

well as a few street scenes. The town has ample subject matter for artists. Years ago, Charles Hawthorne, the famous portraitist, lived and taught painting in Provincetown. Here, Hawthorne established his famous artist colony that attracted many artists from all over the country.

After the workshop, I intended to go to Rockport, Massachusetts. Sovek drew a map to make it easy for me to find my way. He told me to phone his friend, the artist Movalli, who lived in Rockport. Movalli was another artist whose work I admired. Unfortunately, he was on vacation, and I wasn't able to meet him. I painted a few paintings at the picturesque Rockport harbor that many artists, past and present, have painted. I also painted a few street scenes and fishermen's huts around the town. It was a rewarding experience, and an opportunity to paint in a part of the US that was new to me.

During those workshops, Sovek and I developed a friendship that lasted for years. We communicated via email regularly. We also exchanged artwork, and he generously wrote a few words for the back of my book, *Paintings, Drawings and Images in Words*.

On March 30, 2006, I packed my Toyota Sienna with a small suitcase, my trusted full-size Julian French easel, three dozen cotton-canvas panels, my usual oil paint tubes, brushes, and a sketchbook, and drove to Monterey, California, for a weeklong painting spree.

With endless subjects everywhere, I decided to paint quickly and create as many paintings as I could, aiming for an overall impression of the subjects I saw and keeping a blind eye to details. At Point Lobos, I saw crusty gray rocks with splotches of sienna, capped with patchy tufts of moss-green growth. Inlets with glass-like waters reflecting the silvery skies and background blue-gray hills that looked like humps of whales across the horizon, formed a magnificent scene. I placed my easel up on a hill and painted China Cove, a sandy patch with emerald-green waters between tall rocks.

I walked up the sandy hill of Carmel Beach and set up my easel, its legs deep in the sand, and despite the pounding wind, I painted the park and ocean scenes.

I drove to a point overlooking the Carmel Valley sprawled below and did a painting standing by the highway as cars whizzed past me at high speed. In my painting, farmland stretched in the valley into the distance. White farm buildings amid deep-green trees dotted the landscape against a backdrop of gray-purple hills.

Toro Park, close to Salinas, was a pleasant park of gorgeous trees, hills, and trails. There stood hefty trunks of trees with twisted gnarled limbs, their massive arms arched with tips reaching the ground as if their purpose was to hold up the tree.

Along the highway in Salinas, I saw migrant men and women working under the glaring sun, picking strawberries or maybe lettuce. In the evening, I went to a warehouse-sized buffet eatery that had an inexpensive variety of delicious Mexican food. Migrant families, men, women, and children, came to dine after a long day of toil, the adults' necks scorched by the harsh sun.

I have always associated Salinas with my favorite writer,

John Steinbeck. Seeing these scenes and people, I had the urge that when I got home I would reread my favorite novel, *East of Eden*.

Popular in Carmel is 17-Mile Drive along the coast. It is known for its picturesque scenes, cypress trees, and Pebble Beach. I did a painting with my easel perched and balanced on rocks.

I next painted in Moss Landing, a busy fishing port where large charter boats anchored by the dock and small sailboats moored across its length, and there were picturesque buildings in the background. There was so much going on that it required simplified compositions.

I was painting beautiful tugboats in a harbor when a fisherman passed by. Looking at my half-finished painting, he stood for a few minutes before saying, "You don't do this for a living, do you?"

An hour later he came back and scrutinized my painting for a few minutes, comparing it to the scene. "Hey, that's not bad. How much do you want for it?"

Among the lovely parks I visited was the Pinnacles National Park. It had a carpet of California poppies, a blast of vivid orange among white pebbles and larger round stones—an enticing landscape to paint.

By the time I was ready to drive home twelve days later, I had used all the canvas boards I brought with me. It always seems that at the end of a painting trip such as this, I am in a state of self-satisfaction that I have accomplished something worthwhile, but also one of physical exhaustion.

In 2007, I decided to spend a week painting in Bend,

Oregon. Artist John O'Brien, whom I hadn't seen since we were both involved with the Watercolor Society of Oregon, found out about my intended painting trip and asked if he could join me. He and his wife had lived in Bend, and he was familiar with parks and lakes in the area, he said. It turned out he was a great painting companion throughout the week.

Bend is Central Oregon's largest city. The Deschutes River runs through it, which along with the surrounding lakes, is the area's attraction for me. The area has a volcanic flavor as seen by the rocks around the river, and its climate is classified as high-desert, semi-arid. I spent a productive weeklong painting excursion in perfect weather.

My friend and I painted street scenes in the town and landscapes around the Deschutes River, with its waters and its rapids. We spent hours painting at Sawyer Park, where the river cuts through basalt rocks, forming a dramatic rock formation by its bank.

I drove to Smith Rock State Park, about twenty-seven miles from Bend. I set up my easel at the edge of the parking area where I could get a stunning view of the 600-foot massive cliffs looming over the Crooked River that meanders through the canyon. While I stood documenting on my canvas the enormous breathtaking scene, young hikers passed by me on a trek down the steep narrow trail that wound down to the river below that, from my standpoint in the distance, looked like a sky-blue length of yarn, bending and swerving in the deep canyon below.

In 2015, the Bend Art Gallery Association asked me to teach a workshop in their area. For enthusiastic participants, I did a demo of a landscape on a hillside at Sawyer Park as well as a street scene. Subsequently, a newly established gallery in Bend, the River Bend Gallery, gave me a one-person exhibit. In it I displayed many of my oil paintings of landscapes, still lifes, and portraits. It was an impressive show and gave me a presence as an artist in that part of Oregon.

CHAPTER 24

Retrospective, OPB Art Beat, and More

Throughout my artistic career, I was eager to delve into attractive styles of painting. My serious attempts at discovery might span a few months. At some point, it might become clear that such a style suited my temperament, and if not, then I might choose whether to incorporate or adopt the novelty into my own artistic preference or totally discard it, having cherished the experience. In time, my preference for the type of painting and drawing I enjoyed and adopted leaned toward the semi-abstract or gestural and sketchy art. Eventually, I created a large body of work that varied in media and genre, yet still preserved my intuitive primary interest and preference in painting that many identified as my style.

In a retrospective, a major turning point in my career as an artist, my artwork was exhibited at Maude Kerns Art Center's three main galleries—unprecedented for a one-person exhibit. The exhibit featured my landscape, figurative, and still-life paintings, several of my abstracts and drawings done in a variety of media, as well as some of my sculptures.

The following is a quote from Maude Kerns' newsletter: "His paintings are marked by vibrant colors and an exuberant and sensual handling of materials. Candy Moffett, collector and former gallery owner, describes Sarkis in this way: 'Sarkis is an extraordinary gifted and versatile artist, equally facile in several genres from impressionism, expressionism, to nonobjective or abstract art. He is fluent in oil, watercolor, pastel, and ink. His work is treasured by other artists as well as art aficionados. Sarkis Antikajian teaches us all how to 'see' with new eyes.'"

While my retrospective was on exhibit, I received a phone call from Oregon Public Broadcasting (OPB) asking to profile me on their *Oregon Art Beat* television series. The *Art Beat* series is OPB's Emmy award-winning weekly television series that profiles artists, musicians, and artisans.

In May 2009, on a bright spring morning, a film crew from Portland arrived at our place in Cheshire. It must have been around 8 a.m. and an occasional bird song accentuated the quietness of a crisp, cool morning. I had set up my French easel and palette with mounds of my usual cool and warm primary oil colors placed around the perimeter of my easel's folding palette. As soon as Greg, the cameraman, was set up to start the filming, our neighbor's dog, seeing all the commotion across the fence, began barking ferociously nonstop—an unacceptable situation for filming. Our neighbors, alerted to the problem, took their dog inside, and to the producer's relief, the filming began as I stood painting a section of our front yard and part of our home.

As I proceeded to paint the landscape, Greg stood right behind me, his bulky camera braced on his shoulder, moving his lens back and forth from the landscape to the canvas and to the palette, focusing on my brushstrokes and my color mixing.

After I finished the landscape painting, Katrina, the producer, was delighted that I was willing to be filmed doing a portrait of Karen. I led the way up the steps to the second floor of my studio, where I usually paint whenever I am not painting outdoors. The crew followed me, lugging the massive filming equipment up the steps to my workspace, where invariably, like many previous visitors to my studio, they were awed by the ambience of a typical artist's studio—easels and palettes of different sizes, brushes, oil and acrylic tubes on carts, pastels in trays, and watercolor boxes on tables. The scent of linseed oil permeating the studio added to an artistic environment where I feel at home, where the sound of my brushstrokes against the rough weave of the canvas is most invigorating against a soothing Chopin prelude seeping through the stereo speakers. Although to this day I still use linseed and oil paint, I miss the aromatic scent of turpentine that I used until just a few years ago. Most young artists I painted with disliked the odor of turpentine, and out of courtesy, I switched to using purified paint thinner such as Gamsol. For me, turpentine had always optimized what I considered the true artist's studio and workplace aura.

Karen posed, seated on the far end of the maroon couch by the ten-foot picture window. She had one arm over the backrest, and faced me in a pleasant, relaxed pose. Portrait painting requires accuracy in drawing and absolute focus with the least distraction. I have trained myself to work intuitively even when subjected to distraction, which was crucial that morning with the overwhelming pressure of being filmed.

With the camera a few inches above my head, I began

painting. I splashed oil colors of a watercolor consistency over a forty-by-thirty-two-inch canvas, a process I have been using in the initial stage of the painting when placing the figure on the canvas in a satisfactory design. I then proceeded to apply thicker oil paint, modeling the figure. I almost completed the portrait during filming.

At noon, we drove to Maude Kerns Art Center to have lunch. After lunch, the crew filmed me conducting a workshop and doing a demo in a classroom setting for a group of student artists. I painted a still life from a setup of artificial red flowers in a vase with fruit. After that, they did a segment showing me walking through my retrospective and talking about a few of the paintings in the exhibit. Late afternoon, the filming culminated with an interview by Katrina.

Karen and I were present at OPB's headquarters in Portland, watching off camera, when the final episode was filmed. OPB showed Karen's completed portrait on an easel set behind the presenters. The episode aired in November 2009 and spotlighted prominently the wide range of genres and styles I pursued. Throughout the episode, Katrina effectively narrated a synopsis of my artistic career and who I am as an artist.

The following May, OPB invited the public to an open house to learn about their operation and asked me to do a demo at their site in Portland. During that afternoon, while I did the demo for a few interested artists, they had my episode projected on a large screen, running continuously throughout the day.

I had viewed many of the *Art Beat* episodes of other

artists, but none showed such an extensive variety of what the artist did, as in my episode. In only seven minutes, this excellent production covered what I do in my artistic career and at the same time showed an overview of my retrospective at Maude Kerns in an impressive presentation. It was a significant turning point that placed me in a select group of Oregon artists.

Many claim that for artists to succeed in the marketing arena, telling stories about each of his or her paintings is most productive. I have never been able to market my work or tell stories about my paintings, and I have always believed that the painting, not the artist, tells its own story. Nevertheless, especially with many galleries closing, I had to devise a way to have my work seen by the public. And I figured there was no better way than to have some of it in a book.

In 2004, I decided to self-publish a coffee table art book, not realizing the intricacies of such a major project. Garrick, familiar with publication software, put together a tutorial that clarified the complicated process. Compiling a book required a lot of time and know-how. Collecting images in high resolution for printing was a formidable task. Stored in four auxiliary hard drives, I had hundreds and hundreds of images of my work to choose from. Deciding which images to include was a big problem. At some point, it was such an overwhelming process, I decided to forget about it for a while. Months passed. Then Kyle, out of the blue, asked, "Dad, what happened to the book you were working on?"

I immediately got back to it. Since this was a once-in-a-lifetime project, Karen and I decided to publish it in hard copy and on heavy paper. We hired a print broker in Seattle to provide us with a variety of possibilities. And that added to our many decision-making intricacies. We had to make many decisions on every part of the bookmaking process— the quality of the paper, the cover, the spine, head, tail, end papers, and so on.

I included a few of my poems even though I do not consider myself a poet. And now, I regret that I didn't edit my poems or even eliminate a few of them.

I titled the book *Paintings, Drawings and Images in Words*. It has192 pages with 274 images, most in full color. It is an inclusive retrospective of my artistic work—costly but impressive. The books arrived from the printer in March 2007.

At some point in my career, I determined the necessity of having a website where one can visit and see my artwork in a variety of media and painting genre and where I can also show my recent work. I discovered a marketing platform to initiate my art website. With the help of my son Garrick, who is a graphic designer, we chose a template, and Karen took it upon herself to set the website up and upload images. I also provided a monthly email newsletter with my personal theories on painting and art in general, as well as a display of my recent artwork. Soon we found out that the website was cumbersome to maintain. I often had difficulty sending my newsletter via email.

Then we discovered FASO, an art marketing website provider. Garrick helped me find a template that showed my work to my liking. For the plan I subscribed to, there was no limit to the number of images I could post. FASO is a user-friendly website that is easy to maintain on my own. Through my website, I have a newsletter system. I send a monthly email newsletter to subscribers, showing a few of my recent artwork as well as information relating to art.

Although maintaining it is still time-consuming, it seemed to be the only way to share my artwork with the public in an impressive showcase.

CHAPTER 25

Lefkara—An Artist's Painting Paradise

In July 2013, Karen gave me a memorable present: a six-week painting vacation in Pano Lefkara, a small village in Cyprus. I had never been to Cyprus and had never heard of Lefkara.

Lefkara is made up of two villages that are side-by-side: Pano Lefkara is the larger, upper village, and Kato Lefkara is the smaller, lower village. My nephew Gaby and his wife, Sylvia, had spent a few days in Pano Lefkara and brought it to my attention. Gaby and Sylvia have always genuinely believed in me as an artist, to the extent that they decorated the walls of their lovely home in Dallas with quite a few of my paintings. They thought that, since I was a color-oriented artist, the colorful village they discovered would give me ample subject matter to paint.

My trip began with my flight to Gaby and Sylvia's attractive home in Dallas. I enjoyed an evening with them and their Chihuahuas and had a delicious Armenian meal that Sylvia prepared. Early in the morning, the three of us boarded the plane to Cyprus. For quite a number of years, they have flown to Cyprus and Beirut for an annual visit to Sylvia's mom, Ani, in Nicosia and Gaby's mom, my sister Peggy, in Beirut. I have always thought of myself as a timid and a helpless traveler, but accompanied by seasoned traveling companions, my trip to Cyprus was most comfortable.

When we arrived in Cyprus, the three of us drove to Lefkara to check out the apartment that Gaby had booked for me from a Cypriot woman by the name of Pisa. My apartment had a bedroom, bathroom, living room, small kitchenette, and a beautiful veranda with a table and four chairs. Next to my apartment was a most convenient laundry room. It was a perfect apartment for my six-week painting venture.

With the key to my lovely apartment in my pocket, we spent the day exploring the alleys of the village, and we had lunch at a famous restaurant on the outskirts of the village. After that, I was on my own, except for weekend visits from Gaby, who always brought an abundance of delicious pastries and breads that Sylvia had packed for me.

Lefkara is certainly a haven for an artist with its red-roofed houses and cottages dotting hills and valleys, olive orchards, vineyards, fig trees, cacti, and exotic brush everywhere in the countryside landscape.

The village's alleys are narrow yet picturesque, with bougainvillea vines trailing over stone walls, and exuberant tropical flowers in terracotta pots in every courtyard. Old and young artisan women sat along the main road in front of shops, creating the lovely lace that Lefkara was known for. The men, whenever they didn't lounge in cafés, chatting or playing backgammon, engraved intricate silverware.

My daily routine was to wake up around 5 a.m. and have one or two cups of Turkish coffee with a quick breakfast. At around 6 a.m., I began a whole day of sketching excursions.

I did my own cooking and prepared light sandwiches to take on my walks. For the next few weeks, I explored most of the narrow alleys and walked on many of the surrounding roads, one of which took me to the nearby village of Kato Lefkara, where I had a delicious Greek lunch.

The most pleasurable explorations were of the surrounding landscapes with olive and fig orchards and a variety of tropical trees and brush. The gnarled olive trees reminded me of Van Gogh's paintings, in which he depicted their unique gestures. I walked over rugged terrain covered with white lime. My walks went beyond the perimeter of the village, yet it was hard to get lost there—no matter where I mindlessly meandered. As long as the Sotira, a tall hill perched up high in the sky with its tall antenna, a backdrop to the village, was kept in sight, I knew where I was and in which direction to walk. In most areas of the countryside, there were no fences and I hardly saw anyone on my daily treks. In some areas of the surrounding landscape, the ground is pure white. It is said that the word *lefkara* literally means "white hills" in Greek.

Throughout my daily walks, I often wondered if going to a town or a village in Europe that was well-known to artists and tourists would have served me well as an artist. I might have found more exotic places to paint, yet it wouldn't have had the pleasant atmosphere I experienced in this village with its laid-back lifestyle and the freedom to roam its lovely landscapes as I pleased.

The village's inhabitants were easygoing and unhurried. Occasionally, a young person rode a scooter or a motorbike in a manner to show off his skill, or I'd come upon two or three men in what seemed to be a heated argument on the verge of becoming a major altercation, but soon found out it was no more than a show of enthusiasm about how nice of a day it was. Otherwise, the village was a tranquil, peaceful, sleepy place.

I walked to what Cypriots call a supermarket to shop for groceries. It was the size of our 7-Elevens, but amazingly stacked six feet high with everything one needed, from vegetables, fruits, and sundries to hard liquor. Most of what would be available at Safeway in the states could be found in this cramped store. When I got to the cashier, who was a young kid, he was in the middle of a billiards game on his register screen, so I waited for a minute or two until he was done. Then, without looking at me, he commenced to enter my items, which he set aside for me to bag.

Cypriots are wonderful people—fun-loving and with a beautiful outlook on life. They are also most generous. To attest to that, Gaby and I found ourselves stranded in a busy gas station after the Honda he was driving (with 240,000 kilometers on the odometer) broke down. The attendants went out of their way to try to fix it and get us on our way, but to no avail. It was truly a tired car! Gaby called one of his Cypriot friends who drove from Larnaca to pick us up. He and his gracious wife fed us appetizing fish for a late lunch, and we took a dip in the nearby Mediterranean. To add to their generosity, our friends served us dinner that was just as delicious as lunch. We could have stayed for breakfast had we not insisted on moving on to Nicosia in a relative's car, where I stayed the night at Sylvia's mom's lovely home.

Lefkara's mesmerizing landscape of orchards, clumps of yellowish brush, and red-roofed buildings and cottages against lilac hills provided perfect scenes in color and subject matter, fodder for my daily sketching. There are exquisite limestone buildings of varied pale tints in the narrow streets and alleys of the village. In my mind, if super realism is the aim, such a subject is best suited for the artist-photographer. Undoubtedly, such images may be depicted exquisitely in a photo. On the other hand, with painting it is much harder to achieve a similar effect, especially when engaging in the process of painting I do: alla prima, the direct method of painting in one go, rather than the technique of tedious glazing, which may be better suited to painting such a subject.

Painting the bright and high-key landscape wasn't easy to do in the acrylic medium I chose for my painting in Lefkara. Acrylic dries quickly and has the tendency to darken when it dries. It is difficult to emulate the oil medium to produce nuances in grayed high-key colors seen in the stone architecture in the village, in the direct style I had been doing in my paintings. The challenge is to attain a bright and colorful look, keeping the painting in high key without using too much white that can dull the colors and result in an undesirably dense and tired-looking painting.

When I sketched the narrow alleys' architecture, it was difficult to find safe locations out of the way of the occasional motorists. The similarities in architecture also demanded creativity in portraying different alleys. I often exaggerated the colors of the stone walls, and sometimes added a figure or figures for interest to strengthen the design.

My daily early-afternoon walks took me on adventures—climbing a steep hill to the summit of Sotira Hill. Sotira means "savior." I often called it a mountain since, for me, the climb seemed almost perpendicularly steep in certain areas. At every stretch of the winding, uphill, narrow road to the summit, I'd stop to sketch or linger for a while, taking in the ever-changing landscape. In the distance was a background of mountains that transformed minute by minute into many shades of lilacs, blues, pinks, and patches of gold ochre. Along my climb to the summit, it was rare that I encountered anyone, and, except for an occasional distracting noisy flight of a magpie, I was engulfed by the deep quiet and tranquility.

At the summit, there was a small church and a bench on which I sat and viewed the breathtaking landscape of Lefkara sprawled below in the valley as well as Kato Lefkara, the lower village that I hiked to one day through a fenceless and trailless landscape of olive and fig orchards. I had lunch at one of its cafés and found my way back to Pano Lefkara.

From the top of that hill, I envisioned the character of Pano Lefkara and its normal day-to-day relaxed activities. I could imagine the young and old women sitting by their little shops, from morning to dusk, embroidering the lace their village is famous for. I also imagined the occasional motorist squeezing through the narrow lanes.

On the other side of the summit of Sotira is a panoramic view that spans villages such as Kato Drys. It also offers a glimpse of the Mediterranean, and the cities of Larnaca and Limassol can be barely spotted in the far distance on the horizon.

After a long and productive day, I would head back to my apartment, happily exhausted, have a quick supper of leftovers from the day before, or, if I still had energy, scramble eggs or prepare a pot of stew, dumping all sorts of vegetables and potatoes in a pot, or opt to have a light dinner of halloumi cheese, olives, fresh cucumbers, and tomatoes from local gardens. After dinner, I would sit out on the patio with a beverage, snacking on almonds and pistachios, having the satisfaction that I had accomplished my goal in coming to this village.

On weekends, with a map of the island in hand, Gaby and I ventured on drives from east to west, south to north, over the hills and valleys of Cyprus. Gaby tackled the arduous driving through very narrow sharp curves, or over steep dizzying mountain roads where, just when we thought we were the only ones at that elevation, we were suddenly faced with the surprise of our lives, a car barreling down on us from around a blind bend—an unnerving situation. Thank heavens it only happened once, because those narrow mountain roads could hardly accommodate one car, and on the other side was a steep ravine. For those who get car sick, a trip such as that is out of the question.

We explored many villages with musical names such as Agios Amvrosios, Agros, Farmakas, Amargeti, Gouri, and many others—all unique in their ambient beauty and hospitable people. In my stay in Lefkara, I tried to learn a few Greek words, but no one gave me the opportunity to practice. In most cases, everyone answered in fluent English.

The few people we encountered on our village exploration

were friendly and hospitable. At one of the villages, during our endless walks through every side road and alley, we were tired and hot when we stumbled on a home with a beautiful grape arbor that had enticing bunches of hanging lush grapes. A young man was helping a very cantankerous old man, who could have been over a hundred, walking with him from one end of the yard to the other and back as the old man resisted. The old man had a beard hanging down to his waist, reminding me of a photo I had seen of the impressionist painter Camille Pissarro. The man who owned the home came by to say hello. We asked him if we might buy some grapes to quench our thirst. Amazingly, he gave us a huge bunch of grapes, washed and bagged, and he wouldn't take a penny. They were the juiciest and sweetest grapes. From this experience, I got a glimpse of the character of the Cypriots, their generosity, and how they care for their aged.

The old in those villages had admirable stamina. I saw a very old woman, who held a cane in one hand and a heavy bag of groceries in the other, climb a steep, rocky hill, stopping every few feet to take a breath or rest for a few seconds. That's what I call stamina and perseverance. There were so many of these old people around in these villages. I am told that the young go to the major cities to find work and send most of their wages back to their folks in the villages.

Those of us who are interested in every stone in the walls of buildings hundreds of years old may find photography of the stone buildings in these villages very beneficial. A photograph portrays this fascinating beauty, especially if enlarged to show weathered stone patina in detail. On the other hand, those of us who want to envision the life of the inhabitants of these villages must see it with our own eyes and not through a lens. We have to see it in real life to hear the sounds and feel the texture of the stones that formed the homes that have stood for hundreds of years. That's how we can learn what it is that makes one village different from another.

We took an unscheduled short trip to Beirut. By the time the plane rose and leveled off, within half an hour or so, it was time to make our descent and land in another city and another country. When the plane landed, a burst of deafening applause erupted from the passengers. Was the applause to commend the pilot for a perfect landing? Or was it relief that we were safe and sound on terra firma? One has to wonder.

The purpose of our unscheduled trip to Beirut was a visit with my sister Peggy, who lives in Beirut with her daughter Annie. Also present were my lovely niece Helena; her husband, Nadeem; their daughter Mayya; Peggy's husband, Alex; and Sylvia's mom Ani.

We spent the days at Peggy's beautiful home with the lovely garden that Annie took care of. She doesn't know this, but in my mind, it's equivalent in beauty to any exotic park I have seen. It is small but colorful, with a variety of nicely spaced tropical plants, an assortment of fruit trees, and wonderful bamboo clumps.

Peggy spent most of the days cooking and baking delicious foods that I had not eaten since childhood but always craved, and of course they were time-consuming to prepare. At night, I stayed with Helena and Nadeem in Brummana, a cool suburb of Beirut. Helena prepared delicious meals and sandwiches. We had a gourmet breakfast, sitting out on the veranda of their lovely condo that overlooked the city of Beirut and the Mediterranean Sea. What a spectacular sight it was!

Helena took Mayya and me to the Silk Museum in a place called Bsous, which was set in a beautiful garden. Our guide explained in detail the fascinating cycle of silk preparation, demonstrated by displaying the life of the moth, from egg to the voracious caterpillar that feasts on mulberry leaves, and finally to the weaving of silk into its cocoon. Then there were real-life displays that showed in great detail the extraction of the threads from the cocoon and how they are woven into cloth. We were able to witness the whole process right before our eyes.

During the time in the 1950s when I attended the American University studying chemistry, I considered Beirut one of the most fascinating and beautiful cities I had ever been in, and my four years enrolled at the university were the most exhilarating years of my youth. The city bustled with excitement and, at that time, was a crucible of European arts and culture. During those years, I attended concerts, plays, and operas far more than any time since. Now, even with all the turmoil that plagues this city, I still look at it with a lot of affection.

Beaches were crowded even in the middle of the week. Wedding celebrations included sights and sounds of firecrackers that might be disconcerting to an outsider but were a daily occurrence in many areas.

Back in Lefkara, my niece Nazig and her husband, Iain, who lived in England, came for a visit and stayed for a few days in the apartment adjacent to mine. It was a lovely relaxing time of daily breakfasts on the veranda with Cyprus strained yogurt on toast sprinkled with za'atar, halloumi, oatmeal with nuts, and tasty English tea. Then all three of us went off for our walk through the alleys of the village or to hike in the countryside.

In the cool evening and out on the veranda with a glass of ouzo (anise-flavored liquor which added to the essence of Cypriot life), we savored Nazig's delicious Armenian meals.

Nazig and Iain asked me to do a painting demo to show how I do my acrylic color sketches. On the veranda, my swim trunks and T-shirts hanging to dry made a colorful, enticing motif. I placed my 90-pound Arches paper on the veranda table, along with my palette and paint tubes, and did a demo of my laundry line, explaining the process and answering their questions throughout the demo, in the same manner as I had been conducting my demos in my painting workshops.

It was difficult to say goodbye to my Lefkara retreat. All in all, it was a joyous adventure. At some point in all of our lives, it may be necessary to seek serenity away from our own environment and day-to-day routine—something I highly recommend. A trip such as this would be one way to achieve it.

I am so thankful to my nephew Gaby and dear Sylvia for making my trip anxiety-free. Gaby was a fun companion and an excellent driver during our occasional scouting of the fascinating villages of Cyprus. As he had to return home earlier than I needed to, Sylvia accompanied me back to the US, and her travel experience made what would otherwise have been a daunting trip a very pleasant one. I am also thankful to

Ani, her mother, who was a gracious hostess during the days I needed to stay at her home in Nicosia.

When all was said and done, I was ready to go back to my beautiful home in the lovely state of Oregon, to my own studio retreat, to my chosen routine, and especially to my wife, who graciously gave me this gift.

CHAPTER 26

A World of Art

Karen and I had pleasant memories of our European trip of 1992, which concentrated on art, visiting many museums in France and Amsterdam, as well as towns with significant art history. So in the summer of 2015, we decided to make another art-focused trip to Europe. We spent the first eleven days leisurely enjoying the sights, museums, and cafés in Paris. We walked along the Seine, the Tuileries Garden, and the bustling streets of this most desirable city. With our insatiable hunger for art, we purchased multiple day passes to revisit museums again and again, especially the Musée d'Orsay.

We took a side trip to Monet's Giverny, an incredible garden that we had already visited during our 1992 trip. From the entrance, the path we walked on beside the dense bamboo opened a window to an incredible view of the lily pond, the willow trees, the green Japanese bridge, and the garden with the irises and poppies among a profusion of flowers in a multitude of varied species and hues. The present garden, as well as Monet's pink house with green shutters, were faithful depictions of his own creation, which had suffered during the WWII bombing. We marveled at the garden and ponds that were so familiar from many of his paintings.

During this trip, we explored places we hadn't seen on our past trip, such as Auvers, and we spent more time in Arles. In both towns, Van Gogh created most of his stunning work, so we walked in his footsteps. We walked on the streets he had walked on and stood in front of the same buildings, gardens, and wheat fields that may have appeared unimpressive to most viewers but were dear to him. It was almost like he was just a few steps ahead of us.

What was most memorable for me was our train trip to the small town of Auvers, where we had a one-night reservation at the only hotel in town. Some of my favorite Van Gogh paintings were from his time in Auvers.

We took the train from Paris to Auvers on a Monday and arrived sometime before noon. We walked a block and a half to the Hostellerie du Nord hotel, where we had booked a room for the night, only to find it closed. We sat on the steps, our suitcases piled up next to us, hoping someone would come to show us our room. After a long time, Karen decided to find someone to talk to about our desperate situation. While I waited on the steps, just in case someone showed up, she walked a few blocks down to the town center and found a proprietor of a restaurant who made a few phone calls and located someone who would open the hotel at 3 p.m. just for us. It was only later that we found out that Auvers basically shuts down on Mondays and Tuesdays, and the information on the internet was incorrect. During those two days, the whole town is asleep. Even their tourist center is shut. Their primary tourist days are on weekends. It's a town where locals don't capitalize on tourist trade or make a big deal of Van Gogh's presence in their town.

Our elegant hotel hostess eventually greeted us graciously and showed us our comfortable room. She apologized that the dining room was closed but offered to fix us something to eat. Karen had already bought us snacks from a little grocery store that happened to be open. The next morning, after we were served a delicious breakfast in a garden setting, we embarked on our exploration of the town and the surrounding country-side that Van Gogh painted.

Whereas most artists look for paintable scenes—colorful, ready-made compositions that most enjoy looking at—Van Gogh chose the mundane that one hardly gives a second look, such as clumps of grasses. He painted them not only once but several times, turning them into most interesting and intriguing pieces of art. Visiting the sites he painted, one has to wonder how he created something out of nothing.

Astonishing to me is his exaggeration and abstraction, exemplified in *Roots and Tree Trunks*, a painting devoid of a foreground or sky. His rendition focused on trunks and roots bulging off a shaven bank as if the tree were in agony, wanting to free itself.

Many of the subjects he painted in Auvers and Arles hadn't changed much in the 125 years since he lived there. The town hall building in Auvers is still the drab structure adorned with flags that he turned into a beautiful piece of art in his lovely rendition.

The church he painted, a gray stone building, also hadn't changed. Yet in his painting he expressed it in an individual-istic fashion, accentuating and exaggerating shapes and lines, introducing touches of color as he did in its windows, using deep cobalt blue, reflecting the sky.

We stood by the wheat field with the forked road where

he may have set up his easel and painted his famous *Crows Over Wheatfield*, which depicts an intense yellow wheatfield against a deep ultramarine sky while crows, as if indignant of his presence, slide in ominous, erratic, black waves over the field. This wheatfield painting may have been the last painting he created.

Inside Ravoux Inn, we climbed narrow steps to the seventy-five-square-foot room where Vincent spent his last hours on his deathbed, his brother Theo by his side. There wasn't much in it—a bed, a chair, a table with a basin. It was devoid of life, yet in its emptiness, we felt the spirit of his presence in a state of isolation.

In our short visit in this lovely village, we saw much of what Van Gogh recreated in paint in the last months of his short life. We paid a last tribute to this inspiring artist by visiting his and his brother's graves in the local cemetery.

Our six-day stay in Arles was a special and memorable taste of the most significant part of Van Gogh's artistic life, and it culminated our stay in France. In front of the train station, we waited with our luggage for a taxi to take us to our hotel. A taxi arrived and picked up a couple who stood by us. After standing for over half an hour in the scorching sun, waiting, and no taxi in sight, Karen phoned the hotel. Within a few minutes, a taxi showed up to take us there.

We later learned that it was only a three-minute walk from the station to Van Gogh's yellow house location outside the city entrance. The yellow house was bombed out of existence in the war, and in its place is a concrete stand with a poster of his painting *The Yellow House* right where he may have set up his easel to paint this magnificent painting. The building in the background of this painting is still there.

While Auvers downplayed its tourist trade, Arles capitalized on his artistic, productive life during his fifteen-month presence in the town. Everywhere we walked, we were reminded of his presence. As well-known as Arles was because of Van Gogh, it displayed not one of Van Gogh's original paintings. And while Auvers is a quiet town with only a few tourists visiting because of its importance in Van Gogh's life, Arles has the reputation of being the zenith of his artistic life, and so it bustles with tourist trade. Nevertheless, it still was a relaxed city where we could leisurely walk all over its alleys, its parks, and its outskirts. We found posters of his paintings in front of the sites he painted, as well as metal markers with arrows implanted in sidewalks, mapping the positions where he may have stood while painting the various sites in and around the city.

Over the next few days, we followed the markers that mapped Vincent's footsteps, reminding me of the time I was a cub scout in the Armenian Quarter of Jerusalem, when, on our field trips, we were to find arrows written on pavements in chalk that led us to our intended site. In Arles, we walked and walked, following arrows, discovering the places where Vincent stood with his easel, paint, and brushes and recreated in vibrant colors what he saw. In almost all cases, the sites were recognizable from his paintings, despite the invented colors he attributed to the subject that may not have been there. He must have believed his own chosen colors enhanced the character of the subject.

The steps to the bridge where he stood painting *Trinquetaille Bridge* looked the same as when he painted them. In his painting, there is a sapling tree by the steps. At this time, a large tree stood in its place. Could it have been the same sapling?

We were looking for the site of the *Old Mill* painting, another artwork that I have always admired and never tired of viewing in my Van Gogh book collections. It is thickly painted and has an expressive, rugged look. Following the arrows, hoping to come upon the image marker denoting the subject location, we came around the corner where we expected it, but to our surprise, the marker and poster were missing. Yet, having had the image of the painting inscribed in my memory, when I looked across the road at the corner, there the mill was in plain sight: a group of structures on the corner of the paved roads—the bulk of the mill recognizable as depicted by Van Gogh. A man came out on a balcony in nearby building, and informed us, with exaggerated hand gestures, that a car had slammed into the poster stand. This must have just happened, since they hadn't had a chance to replace it.

On our previous trip to Arles, we missed seeing the Langlois Bridge that Van Gogh had painted a few times. We thought this would be our chance to visit it, since it was listed in the brochures of Van Gogh painting sites. But the map lacked directions leading to the bridge. We went to the chamber of commerce to find out how to get there. The man gave us another map and asked if we had a car. (We didn't.) Taking a long look at us, obviously senior citizens, he told us to forget it. It was too far, and the only way to get there was to drive.

Without having any idea as to how far the bridge was, we still had the energy and the will to get to it on foot. We followed the highway shown on the map. After walking for an hour, we came to a fork in the road. At the fork, it was difficult to know whether to bear right or left. Luckily, we were in a rural area with a few homes. We found a woman we thought might be able to direct us to the bridge. She hesitated for a minute, then said in English that it was too far, impossible to walk to. But seeing that we were determined to get there, she indicated the road that would lead us to it. We had already walked a long distance. Why not continue and see where the road would take us? So we walked and walked and walked, through business and industrial areas, and sure enough, there it was: the bridge depicted in his paintings—the Langlois Bridge. Soon, a young couple in a small car showed up. Seeing us on foot, they may have wondered how the heck we got there with no car in sight.

In all our discoveries, I thought of scenarios: what Van Gogh looked like, what type of easel he had, his paint-crusted, out-of-shape paint tubes, and the semi-stiff bristle brushes, which may not have been rinsed in clean turpentine for quite a while and with which he scooped paint and slithered it in globs over his canvas rather than meticulously brushing smooth strokes. As we walked on the ground he stepped on 125 years ago, his shadow tagged along, whether in our minds or in our hearts.

Our next step was Amsterdam. Amsterdam is a large, bustling European city with museums such as the Rijksmuseum (the national museum of the Netherlands), the Stedelijk

Museum, and the Van Gogh Museum. Since we had visited the Van Gogh Museum in 1992, the building had been renovated in 1998 and 1999. It contains the largest collection of Van Gogh's paintings and drawings in the world.

From Amsterdam, we took a bus to our favorite museum, the Kröller-Müller Museum in a park in Otterlo, where we booked a room for two nights. This museum has the second-largest Van Gogh collection in the world, with ninety of his paintings that are absolutely my favorites.

With only a few tourists present, which was unique to that museum as compared to the congested Van Gogh Museum in Amsterdam, we viewed his fascinating paintings at our leisure. We were also able to take photos, something forbidden in the Van Gogh Museum. For added enjoyment and culminating our memorable visit, Karen and I rented bikes and enjoyed a ride on some of the many bike trails in the peaceful forest surroundings—a wonderful, relaxing ending to an inspiring two days.

CHAPTER 27

On Belonging

From childhood through most of my adulthood, I have always been restless—a state to which I cannot attribute any reason. I had a supportive, close-knit family and a peaceful home environment—notwithstanding the brief arguments that my brother and my father had, always at the dinner table and having to do with business decision-making. Their arguments amounted to a few minutes of bickering, dominated by my brother. He had partnered in my father's business and needed to assert his importance in any business venture. The disagreements between my brother and father were usually minor—by all accounts, my brother made most decisions, since it was his idea to abandon the transportation business my father had for years and start a music records and musical instruments sales business. My father went along with this, giving my brother the freedom to manage the enterprise. Still, my father was in charge of financing the business, since he had established a good relationship with banks long before any of us were born. In these arguments, my mother, not surprisingly, sided with my brother. That didn't bother my father. He would look at her and smile.

I never felt a tumultuous experience that caused me distress. However, one problem has always been on my mind. Since early childhood, I felt I didn't belong to the country where I was born, caused by the nagging knowledge that we were minority Armenians among a majority of native Arabs. I cannot base it on any unwarranted behavior toward me or my family. My Arab classmates befriended me and treated me well. The Arab population accepted the Armenians, who had chosen the country as their own and were good citizens. Most Armenians were affluent in the Arab society, having their own businesses, churches, and private schools.

The awareness of being different and not belonging to the majority of the population, of being a foreigner in the country where I was born and spent the first twenty-five years of my life, was like a chronic ailment that I could ease with pills yet was unable to shed, lingering as a persistent sensation that kept gnawing small pieces off my contentment or happiness.

The feeling of not belonging wasn't perceived, thought of, or felt by my siblings, all born in Jordan; my mother, born in Jerusalem; and even my father, an Armenian born and raised in a village in Turkey, who found his way in adulthood to Palestine, then to Transjordan—a country that had nothing in common with his upbringing. It was contradictory to his own culture, religious beliefs, and language. With perseverance and respect for its people, their culture, and their faith, he gained total acceptance from its people. He befriended Arabs of the streets, a few Bedouins of the desert, as well as dignitaries, including the Emir Abdullah I, the great-grandfather of the present King Abdullah II. The country and its people gave him the opportunity to prosper, build a good business, have a good home and, for a while, have a few pieces of land he purchased. He hired Arabs and Charkas (people of Slavic descent brought to the area by the Ottomans) and was accepted as a loyal citizen of the country. He learned the Arabic language as best he could. His thick, foreign, and pronounced accent was of no concern to him or to the Arab population. He assimilated into his new world without abandoning his own Armenian identity or his religious beliefs. Despite the challenges he faced, he never had a reason to live anywhere else. He loved his adopted country and its people and remained a loyal and respected citizen throughout his life.

The United States, the country that I chose to be part of, is a country of many peoples, and I have always felt a true citizen of this amazing country. It was much easier for me to adapt to the American way of life than it was for my father to adapt to the country he chose as his own because of the pronounced differences in language, ethnicity, culture, and religion.

In America, I had the opportunity to become an artist, have a beautiful family, and a lovely home. In this amazing country and among its remarkable people, I have contentment and happiness. And here is where I belong.

CHAPTER 28

Like-Minded Friends

Although over the years I have had many acquaintances, I had only a few like-minded friends whom I admired not only as individuals but also for what they were passionate about. Their passion was for the activity itself, whether it was painting, drawing, or photography. The product for these artists, as it has always been for me, is secondary. Most didn't rely on sales of their artwork to make a comfortable living. They had other vocations that supported their artistic endeavors. For these artists, art was a way of life they couldn't do without. And that was the essence of our friendship.

I met Guido Frick, a German artist, in 1983 at Sergei Bongart's workshop. We immediately developed a close friendship and spent time together whenever we could. I even did a watercolor portrait of him on one of his visits to my room. We were alike in our artistic views, and our thoughts on life in general merged. Although he spent half the year in Germany and the other half in the US, giving painting workshops, only once did I see him in person after Bongart's workshop. One day, out of the blue, he phoned me. He said he was in Oregon in our area and had just seen an exhibit of my work in Corvallis and wanted to pay me a visit. We spent time in my studio, and we had a very pleasant reminiscence of Bongart's workshop. And that was the last time I saw him in person. Nevertheless, our friendship spanned forty years, corresponding via emails almost weekly, sharing our thoughts on art and life in general. We admired each other's style of painting that was founded on the Russian impressionistic style. He remained true to his method of painting while I did the same for a few years after the workshop, but then I often veered into different personal ways of painting and experimenting. At some point my method became intuitive depending on my mood or subject.

Bongart gave scholarships to promising art students in his Los Angeles art school. Sunny Apinchapong was one of the recipients. Then he became one of two teaching assistants in Bongart's Rexburg workshop that I attended.

A few years ago, Sunny was painting with a group of artists in Portland, and he phoned to see if he could visit me here in Cheshire. He stayed with us overnight, and he and I decided to join a plein air group in Roseburg hosted by the Umpqua Valley Arts Association. Our first painting site was at the Colliding Rivers near Roseburg. The rivers and the fabulous surrounding rocks were great subjects to paint. We also painted at the Harry Winston House, where we painted the historic home and the lovely garden. Back home in my studio, Sunny did a watercolor portrait of me, and I did an oil painting of him. He is a dear friend and a prominent artist in the Russian style of painting. We have mutual appreciation for each other's art and have developed a close friendship, connecting with each other every so often.

I knew Steve Cooley, a dear friend, and a passionate painter. We enjoyed each other's friendship and companionship. We agreed on pretty much everything—art, literature, and personal life. He had his own vigorous style of painting that was free and suggestive, avoiding exactitude. His interest was to paint the figurative gesture in an expressionistic manner and not necessarily to paint a portrait.

We enjoyed painting together either at Maude Kerns Art Center, at the University of Oregon open studio, outdoors around Eugene, or on the coast. Often, after a painting session at Maude Kerns, we would have lunch and talk for hours. I enjoyed his companionship, admired his talent, and valued his friendship.

Steve's enthusiasm for painting was infectious. When painting a figure at Maude Kerns, he would have his earphones on and would hum and dance, immersed in his painting and oblivious to what went on around him.

He often visited me at my studio. We would paint a still life from a setup or an outdoor landscape. Twice he gave models a ride to my studio, and it was great to paint the figures, each in our own way.

When I told him I was compiling an art book, he was more excited about the prospect than I was. And when I showed him the published book, he held it in his hand, flipping through pages like it was a treasure he had stumbled on. He wanted two books, one for himself and another for a member of his family.

For a few weeks, Steve did not show up at the open studio figure painting sessions. To my knowledge, he rarely missed a week. And he didn't answer the emails I sent him. He had told me he was retiring from the irrigation job he had had for quite a while. But that wouldn't have been a reason for his absence because he always said he could hardly wait to paint during these sessions.

I happened to see Jim, his boss, at a store and asked him if he had seen Steve. He said Steve had undergone heart surgery.

A year later, I had a few paintings in a show in a local gallery, and at the opening, I asked a woman who was at the show, who knew Steve and lived in Cottage Grove (where Steve also lived), if she had any news about him. I mentioned he hadn't answered my emails for months. She said she would talk to him and let me know. And sure enough, he emailed me. I told him I would love to profile him in my email newsletter if he would send me images of his best work. He said he wasn't successful in photographing his work, so we decided he would bring me a few of his paintings, and I would photograph them myself.

When he brought the paintings, I saw a different person altogether. His cheerful disposition was gone. Instead, he seemed aged and withdrawn. He was frail, had lost weight, and wasn't the Steve I knew.

When I published the newsletter, he was thrilled with his profile. Two weeks later, he emailed and asked my opinion as to which small pochade easel box was best for plein air painting. I told him what I thought worked best for me. I said I had a few different brands, and he was welcome to borrow all of them and try them to decide which he preferred. He never answered, and I have not heard from him since, even though I have emailed him several times over the months, with no response. The odd thing is that for the many years I knew him, I never knew his home address other that he inherited his home in Cottage Grove, a small town south of Eugene.

I met Paul Robitschek at Maude Kerns in the painting and drawing open studio sessions. Although he was a chemist, his heart was in art. I admired him not as much for his paintings or drawings but more for his intellect and his passion for the classics, whether for music, literature, or art.

In our weekly luncheons, during which we would chat about our mutual interests, I never found him boring. Our interests overlapped, and I looked forward to our spending time together with no lull in finding a subject to talk about. He also was particularly pleased and proud that I loved Czech classical music and that Dvořák was my favorite composer.

I did two portraits of Paul, but he accepted only one as a gift—a portrait that showed him as a younger man than he actually was at the time. The other portrait hangs in my studio and shows a bald, lanky man, a cane in one hand and a drawing pad in his other. The painting represents him as I knew him.

He asked me one day to give him a couple of my imaginary watercolors to send to his dear friend in Germany. He thought my watercolors had the feel of Emil Nolde's paintings—presumably his friend was a fan of the German artist.

Bill Kunkle and his wife, Marvel, were our neighbors when we lived on Josephine Street in Eugene. Bill and I became close friends and admired each other's art. Although he worked as an insurance adjuster, photography was his passion. He carried his basic camera, a Pentax K1000, at all times, photographing whatever caught his interest. Even at home, his camera stayed by his side. Our conversations always focused on his own art form as well as on my painting. I appreciated and respected that. He and his wife had so much respect for my passion for painting that they asked me to do portraits of each of them. First, I did a portrait of Bill smoking his pipe, emphasizing his black hair, black eyes, and bushy eyebrows, followed by a portrait of Marvel in a graceful pose, full face with a smile that fit her casual nature.

One day, Bill arranged to photograph and interview the Hell's Angels motorcycle gang, who were staying in a ramshackle house in a dilapidated part of Eugene. He asked me to accompany him. They were a group of tough men and women who had a formidable appearance as a group and as individuals. The men and women wore grimy jeans, heavy boots, and dangling chains with knives in sheaths on their belts, displaying provocative insignia and patches on their leather jackets that portrayed a formidable lifestyle. Bill seemed comfortable talking to them, while I felt out of place. I couldn't help watching one of the men with his twelve-inch knife digging out the grime from under his blackened nails. Nevertheless, the visit was a memorable experience.

When we moved to our home in Cheshire, we lost track of Bill and Marvel for many years. One day, Marvel saw me at the Dairy Queen in Junction City and told me they had moved to Harrisburg, a small town close to Junction City, and she enthusiastically said that Bill would love to see me. And so our steadfast friendship continued as if it had never elapsed.

Since Bill is a World War II veteran, Senator DeFazio of Oregon invited him to visit Washington, DC, as a guest. Bill wanted me to accompany him. We spent a most enjoyable three-day train journey across the country. Our experiences in DC were significant and most memorable. Throughout our tour, we were accompanied by a personal guide. We visited the White House and walked through the same corridors presidents walked through in American history. We visited Arlington National Cemetery. Standing by the vast stretched lines of fallen soldiers, the guide recited historical sad events as tears welled in Bill's eyes. I was extremely moved to think of the young men and women who lost their lives fighting for freedom and justice. We toured the Capitol Rotunda and the National Statuary Hall. Throughout this special trip, as a proud citizen, I cherished experiencing American history. It was a most profound experience I would never have had if it weren't for Bill's friendship.

CHAPTER 29

Painting in Public

Experimenting with paint was a never-ending learning process, a habit that has stayed with me to this day. It means working in a trial-and-error fashion, an activity I won't do in the company of others. Early on in my artistic career, when painting outdoors, I often chose a secluded place to paint the landscape. It wasn't easy to choose a composition from all that was available in nature. It required focus and the fewest distractions.

My confidence built while, with other artists, I painted figures at Maude Kerns Art Center. In time, I trained myself to eliminate the presence of others and all the surrounding activity from my mind. In those sessions, most of the participants were professional artists absorbed in their own work, oblivious to what went on around them. The ability to be decisive in painting a figure in open studios allowed me to include painting figures from life as a subject to teach in my workshops. Figure painting is a difficult subject, even more so when time is limited and you are subjected to participants' questions. I learned not to let any of this have an adverse effect on my focus and decision-making.

When a group of artists, or an art association, asked me to give a workshop and do demos, I said, "Why not?" My passion for painting made sharing my artistic knowledge with students, or even the public, a pleasure. I found doing demos invigorating. That said, in my demos, I chose familiar subjects and not complicated compositions that required uninterrupted decision-making as to the choices I needed to make regarding shapes, values, colors, edges, and the placement of the focal point in the composition to achieve a satisfactory outcome.

Familiarity with the subject I painted allowed me to talk about my decision-making throughout the process. I even encouraged questions from participants during the demos. The more I conducted workshops, the more confident I became. In my demos, I also derived benefits from my teaching. I realized that in talking about the process of painting, I clarified and solidified that knowledge in my mind.

A few of my workshop participants often said they wished I did videos of my painting process that they could watch over and over. So I thought, *Why not?* They would be informative demos of my painting process, done either plein air or in my studio: figurative, landscape, and still-life demos done in oil, watercolor, and gouache. Besides creating a teaching resource, I also presented my artwork in numerous YouTube slide shows that spanned my artistic career.

Creating one-person YouTube videos, especially for one who is not adept at technology or videography, as I am, was a formidable project. The hardest part of one-man video demos was dealing with the iPhone camera, which included the ever-frustrating setup to avoid reflections. The video required talking while concentrating on the painting process. By that time, I had experience doing demos for workshop participants and had the ability to paint and verbally describe every step of the painting process. Yet when I did my YouTube demos, I felt I was talking to myself, and it might be misconstrued by another as odd behavior—even though in my backyard my only audience was curious birds flitting around or a visiting deer wondering what the heck I was up to.

Twice on one hot day, after videoing an extensive plein-air demo, to my dismay I found out that the iPhone camera had quit midway during my demo. I didn't know that in hot weather, if the iPhone heats up too much, it shuts down.

I was lucky one day to have Garrick assist me in videoing a still-life demo, and he kept an eye on the phone. When it quit, I stopped the demo for a minute or two while he took the phone indoors to cool it off, after which we proceeded with the rest of the filming. Garrick's help during that video had another positive advantage for me. I felt I was talking to someone, in this case my son, and not talking to myself. I also was relieved not to worry about the technical part of it.

For the timelapse videos and slide shows, I needed to pick background music to complement the subject. The choices of music I made were of my personal likes, were reasonably priced, and didn't overwhelm the slide show but accentuated the ambience of the type of art presented.

For years, I did demonstrations at the University of Oregon Duck Store's art department during their two-day Tools of the Trade yearly events. Artist students at the university and other local artist shoppers stopped by to watch me do the demo and asked questions about the painting process, or about my preferences in art supplies. Some non-artists came by to say hello. In these demos, I had time to stop my painting activity, chat, and give advice when asked. The subjects I often chose to paint were of pencil sketches, photos I had taken of our garden, or photos from our travels. I found it to be an enjoyable two days that I looked forward to each year.

CHAPTER 30

A Shared Haven

When I look out the picture windows of our home or my studio, I realize how our world has changed over the years. From an unfenced field of ryegrass, our place has become a haven for wildlife. The sapling oak trees I dug into the ground aged along with us to reach over eighty feet tall. And with flower gardens, orchards, and ponds, we created an oasis amid the fields of ryegrass that we call our paradise. Deer and other wildlife roam casually over our place. Years ago, I would have been frantic that deer would devour all our blueberry bushes and wipe out our roses and flower gardens. Now, the deer bed under our grape arbor or in our blueberry patch and, in the orchard, eat the fallen apples that Karen used to shovel into a wheelbarrow and place in compost bins. Deer promenade in our flower gardens, nibble at one seductive petal and sometimes stand by our windows looking at us, maybe thankful for our hospitality.

Many varieties of birds visit us throughout the year to feed at our feeders or take a bath in our waterfalls. In spring, swarms of goldfinch brighten our spirits. Some linger in winter months with faded plumes. They flock to our black oil sunflower seed station. In summer, the lazuli buntings and the western tanager, uncommon in this area, bathe in our fishponds' waterfalls. The stellar jay with its black head and tail and ultramarine and shades of cerulean-blue body, scrub jays, chickadees, towhees, woodpeckers, a variety of finches, titmice, doves, and quail stay with us throughout the year. And of course there are the delightful hummingbirds that whiz by our kitchen window, in case Karen has forgotten them, reminding her to fill up their sugar feeders.

My love for fish goes way back to the years when I was a young boy, and when, with my sister's help, I collected a couple of minnows from the stream in the village where we picnicked. Many years later, an adult but still a boy at heart, I built two outdoor fishponds on our land in Cheshire. The larger of the two measures twelve by sixteen feet and is three feet deep, while the other pond is somewhat smaller. Both include waterfalls rimmed with rocks of all shapes, sizes, and colors. The water flows over slabs of stones, evoking soothing and hypnotic sounds. All this is a far cry from the irrigation barrel, the imaginary stream, and the pond of my childhood. I stocked our ponds with a dozen goldfish and a few koi no more than five inches long. The koi, one a brilliant red-orange and three yellow with black markings, are all, at this time, around thirty inches in length. The number of goldfish have multiplied into the hundreds, most six-to-twelve inches long in a lovely mix of colors—black, blue-gray, reds, and many other indescribable combinations—all a joy to see in the water. When I sit by the ponds as the fish glide through the water, it's a pleasurable sight when suddenly the large koi spring out of the water as whales or dolphins do, then splash back in—a joyous affair to watch.

Added to that are the thousands of mosquito fish that are like the minnows of my childhood in size and appearance.

In the morning when I come to the edge of the ponds with my fish food jar, hundreds of fish, including the large koi, scramble, waiting for me, no different from puppies or kittens. We may be sharing a few of the smaller fish with the heron that shows up every once in a while. However, the fish have plenty of great hiding places in the terracotta tunnels I placed in the ponds and under the luscious aquatic plants and water-lily pads that grow in abundance. There is no way to tally the number of fish we have in these ponds, for they keep multiplying to replenish whatever we may have lost. We just marvel at all of them.

Over the years, we have had a few dogs and one snow-white cat that adopted us. It appeared at our door during snowfall. Camouflaged by a snow-white coat, it almost disappeared in the foot-deep snow. Had it not been for its exquisite blue-green eyes that sparkled like crystal, we would not have seen it. It was deaf. When our dog, Anoush, barked at it, trying to dissuade the intruder, the cat ignored her. That's when I called it Dumb Cat. I presumed the cat belonged to one of our neighbors. Yet it stood by the door and wouldn't leave.

"What shall we do?" Karen asked.

I was at a loss. I waited for hours, hoping the cat would leave and go back to where it came from. But it didn't.

"We can't leave it out," I said, "but if we let it in, it will never leave." So I shut the door and waited for two more hours. It was getting dark by then. Reluctantly, I opened the door, and it moved in. We fed it warm milk, and it took over our lives.

Dr. Moye, our veterinarian, checked it out. He said it was

definitely a "she" and a healthy young cat. I had never been a cat lover, and neither was Karen. Actually, Karen was allergic to cats. When we lived in Eugene, one of her pupils gave her a kitten. When she brought it home, Karen was miserable with weepy eyes and a runny nose. She had to take the kitten back, much to the boy's dismay. With our Dumb Cat, it was different. Karen wasn't allergic to her. So the cat became part of our household for years. On spring nights, she preferred to stay out in the yard, in a protected area with Anoush. By then, the two had become friends.

I woke up around 2 a.m. one day and turned on the light in the kitchen, expecting Dumb Cat's usual appearance at the sliding door of the dining room, staring at me, wanting to come in. That's when I would bring her in and feed her. That morning, I was planning to drive to a park in Eugene to paint. I looked through the sliding glass door. She wasn't there. I kept looking every few minutes. Still no cat. Then at daybreak, I looked out the door. Dumb Cat was curled up by the side of the door. I wasn't about to wake her up and bring her in. So I forgot about her. When Karen woke up and came to the kitchen, she asked, "Where is the cat?"

Joking, I said, "The Dumb Cat is taking a long nap or else she's dead."

And I went on my way to the park to paint.

When I came home, early that afternoon, Karen met me at the door. "She died," she said.

For a minute, I stood perplexed by what I heard. I had already forgotten about the cat. Then it dawned on me. It's the cat she is referring to. I couldn't believe it. I went to the door to look at the spot where I last saw her.

"I buried her," Karen said. She had dug a deep hole in our backyard in a spot close to the butterfly bush. On top of the cat's grave, she placed large rocks that she found stacked in the corner of our yard, leftover from my stone wall building project.

Over the years, Dumb Cat and our dogs brought me companionship and affection no human could provide. I have always said in jest that I would rather have a dog as a friend than a human.

We were living in Gallup when I first wanted to get a puppy. I had to convince Karen to accept a dog in our lives, since she'd had no exposure to pets in her childhood. Eventually, she took to the idea of having a dog. The boxer breed was my choice because of my fascination with the proud look it projected. The only boxer I had seen in the past was when I was around eight years old, at the home of a man we visited in Jerusalem. And ever since, the boxer breed fascinated me.

During the long drive to Scottsdale to pick up the puppy from a family who placed an ad in a dog magazine, Karen had warmed up to the idea of having a pet, and the closer we got to our destination, our excitement and anticipation built. We adopted an irresistible male boxer puppy we named Asniv Takavor, meaning "gentle king" in Armenian, and shortened it to Tucky.

He turned out to be a gentle, friendly dog and a delightful companion for both of us, and Karen developed a strong attachment to him. Unfortunately, he was a roamer. We found out that this was a trait of most boxers. At no time could we leave him off the leash. We both had full-time jobs, and in our absence, Tucky had to be chained. When we moved to Oregon, and eventually to our home in Cheshire, our intention was to let him be free, since we lived in the country, hoping that he would eventually settle down and get in the habit of staying around our home.

His gentle disposition toward humans did not transfer to other animals or birds. One of our neighbors, Mr. Hibbard, whom I had not yet met, came one day on horseback to say hello. Tucky watched them approach us. Suddenly he went after the horse, trying to bite his hind legs. The horse kicked, throwing the dog in the air. He flipped two or three times, shook his head, and went after the horse, again attacking him relentlessly. Our neighbor, caught by surprise, tried to retreat. It also took me by surprise, and with little time to think, I lunged at the dog to get hold of him, taking a big chance of getting bit, let alone the risk of being kicked by the horse.

This, among other instances, made us realize that freedom was not possible for Tucky. He had to be chained, especially when we were at work. I built him a doghouse to which, in our absence, we tethered him with a twenty-foot chain.

At one point, we thought of getting another puppy, hoping it would keep Tucky company. In the newspaper's ad section, we found adorable mixed-breed eight-week-old puppies. Our pick of the litter was Pepsi (a name given to him by the children who owned him). Adorable was an understatement. He was a jet black, lovable, and feisty pup—we just could not resist. In no time, he was in Karen's arms on our way to our home to be introduced to Tucky.

It was such a relief that Tucky got along beautifully with our new addition. Pepsi, on the other hand, was a mischievous little mutt. He nipped at the boxer's flappy lips and harassed him endlessly. This may have been his way to play, but his razor-sharp teeth bloodied the poor boxer, who was getting old. As I understood, in nature, such behavior toward the pup's mother would have elicited a sharp nip to put a stop to it. But Tucky showed no hint of aggression toward this new intruder. He would move away if that was at all possible. In a couple of weeks, they got along fairly well, and Pepsi was a good pal and distraction for Tucky in his lonely hours in our absence.

As Tucky aged, he had severe, chronic eye problems. I would take him to the vet, who would stick a needle in Tucky's eyeball. It was a horrible situation that I couldn't stand. The affliction got worse to the extent that the dog was in misery. We were torturing the poor dog with this horrible remedy with no possible cure. So we put him to sleep and had him cremated.

Three of our dogs have broken my heart. The first was Tucky with his eye ailment and the torturously unsuccessful treatment we subjected him to. We lost Pepsi to an unexpected, tragic death I could not forget and grieved over for days—even to this day.

On stressful days at the pharmacy, I looked forward to coming home and being greeted by my wife, Tucky, and Pepsi. One summer evening, I drove the twenty-five-mile trip to our home, relieved from the chaotic atmosphere of a full day at the pharmacy. This was a time of reflection, a time to be thankful for whatever gave me joy and happiness—a comfortable home, my wife, Tucky, and Pepsi. The lovable black mutt would greet me every evening on my arrival, with his tail wagging and swirling in a circle, so happy to see me, as Karen watched with delight. And I savored those moments.

The sky was clear, and dusk was near, and I was relieved to be near our happy home. As I drove slowly around the corner, my glimpse of hope was shattered by an unexpected bump. Sudden fear shot through my heart. I looked in the mirror. *Oh God, what have I done?* My midnight pup, paws flailing in the air, tried to move, in vain, to greet me one more time, or lick my face to make it all go away. I looked in his eyes. Helplessly, I watched blood drain from his mouth. His eyes fading slowly. I carried him in my arms with tears in my eyes as the warmth of his little body drained into mine. Deep in the ground, I placed him gently on his side as the moonlight shone on him for one last time.

Kaj was the last dog we had. He was with me everywhere I went. As soon as he saw me pick up my wallet or heard the keys in my hand, he would race to the door, look at the door knob, then look at me, "Come on, hurry up, let's go." Once outside he raced to the van and jumped into his crate. He happily waited or slept while I got in and out of the van, running errands. Sometimes, I took him to Starbucks, and we sat outside while I drank my coffee. Children and adults came by and asked to pet him. One day, a young woman with long blonde hair came by and asked if it would be okay to pet him. As she showered him with kisses, her hair covered his head. When she stood up, I happened to look at him and saw something small and shiny I could barely see between the tips of his black lips. It was her gold earring he had pulled out from her earlobe.

While I painted in my studio, Kaj watched every move I made. I always wondered what he thought I did or the worth of it all. Then as soon as I sat down to take a break, he would be at my knees, tail wagging, wanting to play.

Early one morning with the energy and frisky playfulness of a pup, he chased a cat, half-heartedly, as usual. We drove to a nursery to buy some flowers. When we got back home, he got out of the van and lay down a few feet from me, watching me plant my flowers. After a while I wondered why he wasn't pestering me as he often did to check on my progress. That morning he didn't. He died—eyes open as if he were looking at me. He was only eight years old. While I dug his grave by the edge of a group of rhododendrons, I sobbed, and then for many days, I grieved every minute I thought of him.

Karen and I decided: no more dogs.

I often imagine Kaj next to me, filling a fleeting loneliness. He gave me all I needed, and he expected little in return. My loyal friend till the end.

Except for Tucky, the rest of our dogs, Mitzi, Anoush, Pepsi, and Kaj, are buried on our land. I would like to tell Karen, if I pass on before she does, which most likely I will, then sprinkle my ashes on top of the hill in the walnut grove or by a rose bush. I would be close to our luscious gardens, along with our dogs and cat, and have an overview of the most spectacular distant landscape. There is no better place on earth for an everlasting repose.

Karen and me in the garden, 2010

House, 2012

CHAPTER 31

Can I Say: "I Am an Artist"?

At the time of this writing, I am over ninety years old. I think of the day, fifty-six years ago, when Karen and I stood on top of the hill of a fenceless rectangular six-acre piece of land, lost amid fields of grasses, the landscape stretching for miles, backed by bluish-green hills on the far horizon. We built our dream house there. Had I known what building a house from scratch would entail, I wonder if it would have remained an unfulfilled dream. But with relentless drive and perseverance, we built our home and landscaped our bare piece of land. We created a place that exudes a state of contentment and joyfulness.

Since I was in my teens, being an artist had been my secret identity for many years. Throughout my pharmacy career, I guarded that secret within me, not daring to expose it to others. Yet in my mind, I lived it day-by-day.

When I retired at sixty-two, a new way of life opened up and beckoned me to follow with abandon a path toward a shining light far, far away. Its glitter sometimes faded in my eyes. I was entrenched in a hopeful artistic life but reluctant to tell anyone loud and clear that I was a painter. Hardly anyone would have believed me. Could a pharmacist become an artist overnight? If it were a hobby I had taken up in my retirement as something to keep me busy, to relieve me of an old person's boredom, they would have taken it as a legitimate and suitable activity. But going at it as I have, putting in hours struggling to learn the craft, sacrificing any leisure time that one would expect in retirement, would have been unheard of.

I admit, it has been a struggle. I often failed to grasp the essence of painting. Small successes would lift my spirit and tingle my body, a promise that I may be on the right track, and I would keep staying the course.

Now, twenty-eight years after the day I retired, I ask myself if I have become an artist. I find myself lost amid thousands, all over the world, who possess that same wishful dream. At this time in my life, it doesn't matter whether I am an artist or someone still hoping to be one. It makes me wonder, had I passed on at sixty-two, when my artistic life had just begun, if my dream would have been unfulfilled and wasted. Yet I lived. In my tenacious pursuit, sometimes unapologetically, I called myself a painter, but hardly an artist.

Off and on I have asked myself what it means to be an artist. Is it when art in a painter's life becomes a relentless quest for a way of life that consumes the mind and body, knowing well that the reward might be minimal, and success a mystery? If so, I can say, "Yes, I am an artist."

Acknowledgments

A warm thanks to my sons: Kyle, who encouraged me to follow through with my writing and publishing my story, and for his invaluable contribution to the book title (he was the one who first mentioned the inclusion of the word *odyssey*); and Garrick, who was always there for me when I needed his knowledge to navigate through the overwhelming computer technology. I treasure his genuine belief in me as an artist.

To Karen, my lovely wife and companion of sixty-three years, I am forever grateful. She stood by me while we built our lives together and never questioned the many paths I took regardless of how outlandish they may have been. Without her, reaching my goal of becoming an artist would have remained an unfulfilled dream.

My appreciation to Donna Galassi, KN Literary Arts' author relations manager, who introduced me to members of KN Literary group, and to Sheryl Zajechowski, who took Donna's position when she decided to venture onto another path. I felt a close friendship with Donna, who showed sincere enthusiasm for my story.

To Kelly Bergh for cleaning up my manuscript, telling me what parts to take out and which to keep in. She said as a memoir, my manuscript at ninety-five thousand words was too long. So I cut it down to forty thousand. "That's too short," she said. So I chose a happy medium.

Heartfelt thanks to concierge Elisabeth Rinaldi. She copyedited my manuscript. Her sincere encouragement and support for my story was invaluable. And during our early morning chats on Zoom, she cheerfully answered my tedious and endless questions and helped me cope with the self-publishing quagmire. Through it all, I felt I have known Elisabeth for years.

To Christina Thiele, who did a marvelous job designing the cover of my book, and put up with all the indecisions on my part to pick one, and only one, among the many impeccable designs I had to choose from.

To Karen Sommerfeld for her thorough reading of my manuscript, looking for the small and large faults and offering her most helpful suggestions to make this book the best it could be.

To C. J. Redwine for her marketing expertise. Her words on the back cover are humbling.

And to my friends Sunny Apinchapong, Wyatt Burger, Chrissie Forbes, Guido Frick, Mike Thoele, and Robert Young, who took time to read my manuscript and offer their personal thoughts on my story.

About the Author

Sarkis Antikajian, born in 1933 to Armenian parents in the Middle East, embarked on a transformative journey that led him to the United States in 1958. After a distinguished thirty-five-year career as a pharmacist, Sarkis  realized his childhood dream of becoming an artist and transitioned into a nationally recognized and award-winning professional painter.

With his Cheshire, Oregon, studio as a creative haven, Sarkis masterfully wields oils, watercolors, pastels, inks, and even clay, bringing to life a diverse array of subjects. His artistic repertoire spans figurative, landscape, still life, and abstract pieces, showcasing a depth of skill and versatility.

Sarkis's captivating works graces galleries and private collections across the United States and overseas, reflecting his profound impact on the art world. For a closer look at his portfolio, visit sarkisantikajian.com, YouTube (@sarkisantikajian9834), or Instagram (@sarkisantikajian).

Sarkis is also the author of a coffee table book of his art: *Paintings, Drawings and Images in Words*.